# GOLF COURSES OF
# HAWAII

*"There is no other place in the vacation world where the traveling golfer is so clearly King!"*

*(left) The fabulous 17th at Mauna Lani, surrounded by lava.*

A Kevin Weldon Production

First published 1991 by CollinsPublishersSan Francisco
A division of HarperCollins*Publishers*

In association with Weldon Publishing
A division of Kevin Weldon & Associates Pty Limited
372 Eastern Valley Way, Willoughby, NSW 2068, Australia



Library of Congress Cataloging-in-Publication Data
Ramsey, Tom.
Golf courses of Hawaii / Tom Ramsey : photography by John Knight :
foreword by Robert Trent Jones, Jr.
p. cm.
ISBN 0-00-215938-4
1. Golf courses—Hawaii—Guide-books.
2. Hawaii—Description and travel—1981—Guide-books. I. Title.
GV975.R36 1991
796.352'06'8969—dc20 90-27608

Editor: George Fuller

Designer: Charles Taketa Graphic Design, Inc.

Typeset in Goudy Old Style

Printed and bound in Singapore
by
Toppan Printing

# GOLF COURSES OF HAWAII

TOM RAMSEY

Photography by JOHN KNIGHT

Foreword by ROBERT TRENT JONES, JR.

CollinsPublishersSanFrancisco

*A Division of* HarperCollins*Publishers*

# TABLE OF CONTENTS

KAUAI
NIIHAU
OAHU
MOLOKAI
MAUI
LANAI
KAHOOLAWE
THE HAWAIIAN ISLANDS
HAWAII

# AUTHOR'S ACKNOWLEDGMENTS

This book is dedicated to author Dan Jenkins and to former U.S. P.G.A. champion Dave Marr, both of whom introduced my wife Carmel and me to Hawaii, specifically to the most abundantly verdant island on Earth, Kauai; to Harry Trueblood, Jr., who entertained us royally at Princeville for so many years.

My appreciation also to Bob Holden and to Bill Mielcke who extended the aloha spirit to us so often, Bob at the Royal Hawaiian and Bill on the Big Island of Hawaii, first at Kona and later at Mauna Kea.

The six golfing islands of the Hawaiian group are, reading from northwest to southeast, Kauai, Oahu (where Honolulu sits), Molokai, Lanai, Maui, and the Big Island of Hawaii, and the golfing chapters will follow that route.

If it sounds a bit bewildering, geographically, it is anything but. Inter-island travel is encouraged and flights to any of the so-called "neighbor islands" from Honolulu Airport are frequent.

In fact, what is wonderful about a holiday in Hawaii is the ease of movement from resort to resort, with their manicured fairways and superb golfing facilities. Those who do not play golf can while away as many hours as they wish at swimming, beachcombing, sunning, volcano climbing or trekking through lush rain forests.

But one point quickly becomes clear at the very beginning of a Hawaiian holiday—there is no other place in the vacation world where the traveling golfer is so clearly King!

Tom Ramsey
September, 1990

Soft afternoon light on Princeville's Lake course, 9th hole.
One of Robert Trent Jones, Jr.'s magnificent Hawaii designs.

# FOREWORD

When Tom Ramsey extended me the honor of writing the foreword for this magnificent new volume, I jumped at the opportunity. You see, the Hawaiian Islands are still "Paradise on Earth" for me. I have a home on the beach at Hanalei, close to the 45 holes I created at nearby Princeville. I never expect to find a more beautiful place on Earth on which to build a golf course. As much as I travel, Hawaii is more often than not on the itinerary. Strangely, it even works out that way sometimes when I am actually headed in the other direction!

It wasn't too many years ago that thoughts of the Hawaiian Islands brought to mind the old Matson ships, pineapples, and sprawling sugarcane fields. Now, when the islands come to mind, you are apt to think of places with exotic names like Mauna Kea, Kaanapali, Princeville, Waialae, or Waikoloa – places known as much for golf as for anything else. Such has been the rapid evolution of golf in Hawaii since the jet airplane made its appearance in the late 1950s.

I take pride in the fact that the Jones family had something to do with the explosive growth of the game in the islands. First, it was my father who built the beautiful Kaanapali North Course on the island of Maui. Later, I was fortunate enough to work as his apprentice at Mauna Kea on the Big Island. There, we revolutionized golf course construction, actually creating topsoil by pulverizing lava rock. Since then, and over the past 20 years, I have been privileged to put my signature on seven splendid golf courses in the Hawaiian chain. So is it any wonder that I have such an affection for this glorious little piece of the world?

Golf in Hawaii started at a slow pace, begun by a handful of hard-working Scots who were among the islands' early settlers. These hardy folks have two passions in life: the beverage that bears their name and the game of golf, not always in that order. So, it was not so unusual for little nine-hole layouts to pop up among the big plantations, such as Honokaa on the island of Hawaii. The Oahu Country Club was the first private club in the islands, and, of course, the military bases have always built golf courses as part of their recreation programs.

When you talk about golf personalities in Hawaii, the first was Alex Bell, who arrived in Honolulu in 1912. Alex came from his native Scotland as the first golf professional at Oahu Country Club, and he remained the only professional in Hawaii until Ted Benedict arrived in 1927 to prepare for the opening of Waialae.

Alex's son Art became the head professional at Maui Country Club when he was only 19. Later he became a fine player on the U.S. pro tour and eventually the resident professional at the famed Pebble Beach Golf Links in California.

There are many great personalities in the history of golf in the islands. For years, in the old Crosby Tournament at Pebble Beach, the team of Francis H.I. Brown and Ted Makalena was the official Hawaiian entry in the annual clambake. "Uncle" Francis was a world-renowed amateur player and Ted was probably the greatest golfer ever produced by Hawaii.

To those mentioned above, add the likes of Dick Knight, Guinea Kop, Walter Nagorski, Jimmy Ukauka, Art Armstrong, and Kenny Brown. This book should be dedicated as a living monument to them. For they are among those who built the very foundation on which the game is played today in the proud State of Hawaii. They certainly prove that the short grass of Hawaii's golf courses is just as important to the state's economy as the tall grass of its sugarcane fields.

Personally, my work in the islands has been a labor of love, and I suppose it will be that way the rest of my life. I may not be a permanent resident at my beach home in Hanalei, but my heart is always there. I often dream of playing the championship Princeville course and the majestically beautiful and challenging Prince course nearby.

I am sure you will enjoy this Tom Ramsey masterpiece as much as I have, since it combines the greatest game in the world with the beauty of the Pacific paradise we all love so much.

For you island folks, consider yourselves lucky. For all you others, come visit us soon. Aloha!

Robert Trent Jones, Jr.
August, 1990

ISLAND OF

# KAUAI

Kauai, the Garden Island, is perhaps the most abundantly verdant island on Earth.

Captain James Cook first made landfall at Waimea on Kauai's west side in 1778, and since that time the island has drawn settlers from the outside world who gave in to the spectacular beauty and the unique way of life, and stayed.

There were whalers who jumped ship in this paradise, Russian adventurers who planted grapes and re-named the Hanalei Valley in honor of the Czar, and New England missionaries who came to save souls and "educate" the Hawaiians.

Other settlers tried to strike it rich with coffee plantations, silk-making operations and with one of the grandest sugarcane mills ever assembled in Hawaii. In the end, it is fair to say that Kauai's beauty remains its brightest asset.

*Kauai's famed Na Pali coastline.*

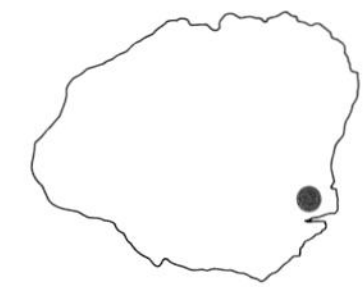

# KAUAI LAGOONS

There are two Jack Nicklaus-designed courses at Kauai Lagoons, adjoining Lihue airport: the Lagoons course (6,942 yards for those who like to manage a few pars) and the Kiele course, which, at 7,070 yards, will arduously test any low handicap player.

The opening holes of the championship Kiele course make you ask, "What's so difficult about this layout?" You soon find out. It gradually becomes tough, then brutally so, with strategically placed bunkers, tighter fairways and more slope to each succeeding green.

It requires length, accuracy, and a sense of touch on the putting greens. The front nine includes two pretty tough par threes and two par fives that just might be reachable for the long hitter. The back nine provides golfers with some lovely scenery. Number 13, for example, is a 207-yard par three, where both the teeing ground and putting green are built into rocky cliffs with ocean surf pounding on the shore some 80 feet below.

This is a lovely site. Both course layouts stretch into deep, dark forests, sweep past palms, and, for an instant, border churning surf. The only irritation is the occasional roar of jet engines as they take off or pull to a halt at Lihue. Nicklaus obviously likes the idea of staging a major tournament on the Kiele course, hence the spectator mounding which flanks each fairway.

Differing in style from the Kiele, Nicklaus incorporated some Scottish-type bumps and hollows on the Lagoons course. It has generous and gently rolling fairways and well-contoured greens.

Both courses are wrapped around the 580 acres of the spectacular Kauai Lagoons, the largest man-made lagoon in the world, featuring seven islands which are home to flamingos, crowned cranes, wallabies, and various exotic wildlife. The Westin Kauai hotel also sits on the property.

In the distance, the Kilohana Crater and Haupu Ridge add a dramatic backdrop for your rounds of golf.

*(left) Kauai Lagoons is a visual treat. Here the 9th fairway is bathed in yellow light.*

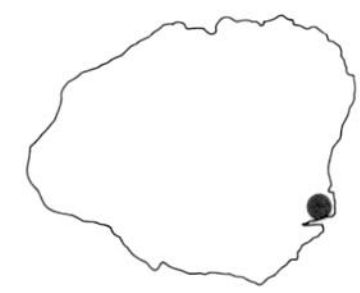

# THE LAGOONS COURSE

The Lagoons course was designed in the Scottish links style with an abundance of wide, rolling fairways and well-contoured greens. It is a course which allows less accomplished players to hit away without trepidation.

"Our goal was to create a course where players would have plenty of room to hit the ball," Nicklaus said, "and still find some exciting golf."

The Lagoons course is not as dramatically beautiful as its sister Kiele, in that it does not have the stunning ocean vistas and cleverly designed layouts. Nevertheless, the setting is still Kauai. And the Lagoons course can provide a moderate challenge and a fun-filled round of golf.

*(left) The 14th green of the Lagoons course. Go easy, or you could be washed up!*

*Featured Holes:*

## Hole 3 - 147 Yards Par 3

The green is in the shape of a dog bone, with bunkers contributing to the narrowing of its waist, and it lies diagonally from near left to far right. Across the narrowest part is quite a severe slope, making the right rear portion of the green considerably higher than the left front. The water hazard, and it is sizeable, comes in at the left, on the leeward side. To make all this easy on yourself, hit an authoritative 6-iron (one longer than it looks) and bend it in from the left, against the wind, but into the length of the green.

## Hole 5 - 407 Yards Par 4

Play the tee shot keeping in mind the cross wind from the left, which also has a tendency to hold the ball down. The best idea is to keep left and aim for the water hazard which guards the left side of the green. The bunkering on the left side of the 4th hole is now common to this fairway. The bunker complex is vast and if you are not very accomplished in getting out of sand you may be here for some time. A mid-iron, depending on the breeze, should suit your second shot. There are mounds and a bunker on the right and one bunker on the left, designed to keep your ball out of the water that crosses in front of the green. The green is only 20 yards at its widest, but it is 50 yards deep. In other words, this green is long and lean.

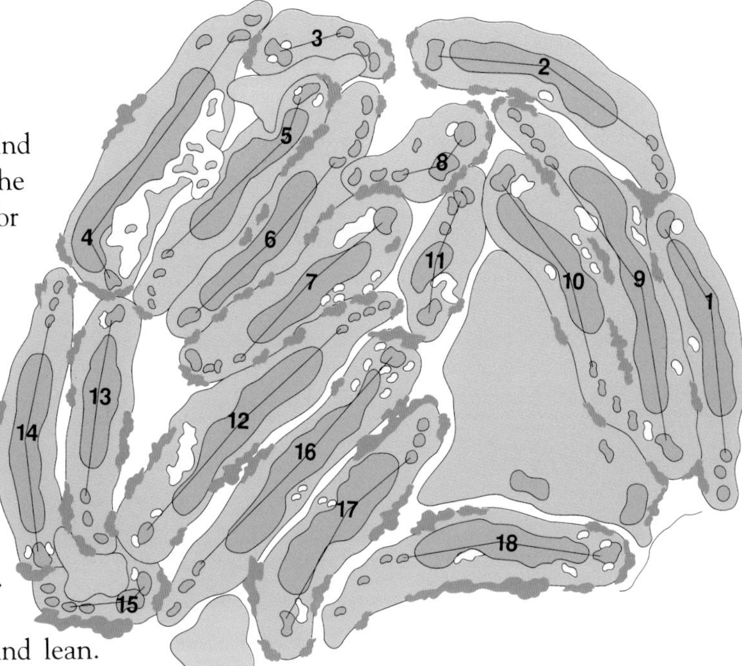

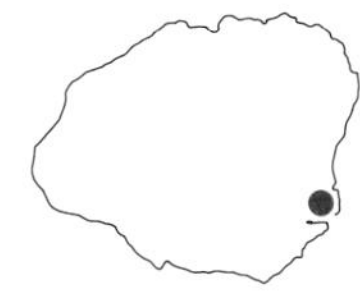

# THE KIELE
## COURSE

Translated loosely, Kiele means "the sweet fragrance of the gardenia." With its spectacular scenery and design excellence, the course is indeed a sweet-smelling flower.

At least you might feel that way until you play a round. Because the Kiele course can be devilishly difficult, particularly on the back nine. The greens are placed to require accuracy from the fairways — and there are plenty of hazards to which it is easy to become victim.

Each hole features a piece of art as its tee-marker: large marble sculptures on 6,000-pound granite bases. You'll find yourself observed as you tee off by a dragon-turtle, a graceful swan, a laughing Buddha — and, on the 18th, a golden bear. Sometimes you wonder if the golden bear is laughing, too!

*(left) The 5th tee at Kiele requires 200 yards of carry over this deep gorge to make par three.*

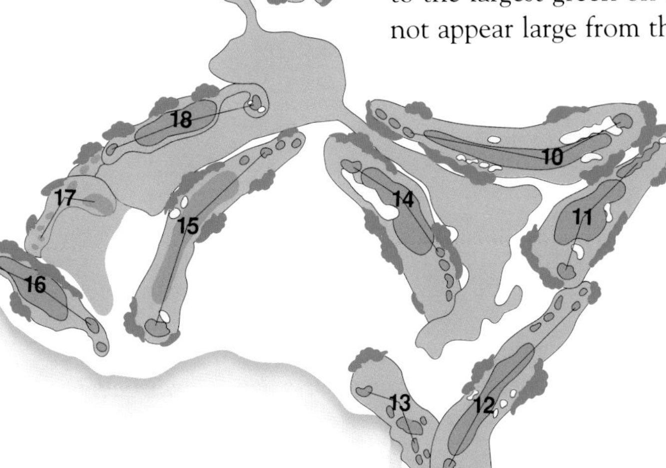


*Featured Holes:*

### Hole 5 - 219 Yards Par 3 – *The Eagle*

Over a mango, guava, and plum forest, you come to the largest green on the course, although it does not appear large from the tee. Be sure to keep your ball in the air for the full distance. Enjoy the beauty of this hole before or after, but certainly not during the long iron in to this split-level green.

*(above) A wedding chapel graces the lagoon's far edge on Kiele's 17th.*

## Hole 10 - 562 Yards Par 5 – *The Hippo*

This dog-leg left hole is definitely a three-shot hole into the prevailing wind. Even though the water on the right is beautiful, it is still a hazard. Aim your driver to the bunker on the left and let it drift back to the middle. Between the right side of the fairway and the water hazard there is also a collection of bunkers. Avoid them as best you can. At this point you still haven't quite reached the dog-leg, so take advantage by having a look at where you'll be going from the point on the right edge of the fairway. Then, take a 3-wood and beam it straight at the radar antenna in the distance, leaving all the sand on your left. For your third shot to the green, which is perched up a little, from about 105-110 yards out, it looks like a 9-iron. Forget it. Hit a full 7-iron into the breeze, the green will take it.

## Hole 13 - 207 Yards Par 3 – *The Frog*

Don't let the distance scare you, because you can use the prevailing right- to-left tradewinds. The green also runs its length in the same direction. Forget the fact that you are shooting over the ocean, and confidently hit your 3-iron, coming in from the right, and land it on the two-level green.

*(above) The 8th is a par three, 169-yard beauty.*

## Hole 16 - 330 Yards Par 4 – *The Turtle*

The first of a triad of great finishing holes, don't let the rating of 18 fool you on this one. It is not that easy. From the tee, you see coconut palms left and right and the first part of the fairway. That is all. Without any trepidation, hit your 3-iron solidly down the middle. You are now confronted with a downhill, unforgiving shot if you pick the wrong club or hit it offline. The green is sitting out on a small peninsula, next to a lighthouse. Don't feel nervous when you line up your wedge shot.

## Hole 18 - 431 Yards Par 4 – *The Golden Bear*

The Golden Bear – Jack Nicklaus – says this hole is one of the strongest par fours he has ever designed. It is into the prevailing winds and plays longer than its yardage indicates. There is water the entire length along the right, but there is a generous landing area for your drive and that is all the leniency you are going to be shown. It's decision time. Apart from a narrow neck of land coming from the left, the target area is an island, and a good 3-wood is needed to carry the water and bunkers to make the green, which is girthed by palms. The alternative is to lay-up short of the water with a 7-iron and then hit a wedge onto the green, hoping for a one-putt par.

*Kiele's 11th: Nicklaus designed a wide fairway with lots of inviting sand.*

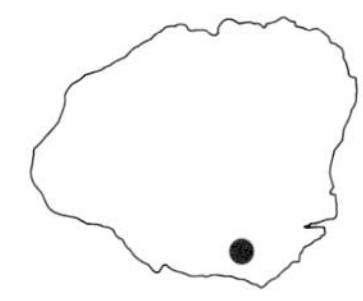

# KIAHUNA
## GOLF CLUB

The Kiahuna Golf Club, located at Poipu on the sunny south coast of Kauai, provides a good test of the game for visitors to the leeward side of the island. It is a shortish, 6,358-yard layout with its fairways well above the sea, but the par is 70 and requires most shots to be in the bag.

*(left) On Kauai's sunny south side, Kiahuna provides golfers a relaxed setting in a rural environment.*

The lava rock formations are placed strategically around the course, and the rolling terrain, an abundance of hidden traps, devilish mounds, and well-contoured greens are certainly a trademark of its designer, Robert Trent Jones, Jr.

Some 100 bunkers guard the fairway landing areas, while the aforementioned mounds often pop the shot onto a hanging lie. Three lakes, a stream, and green mountains add to the course's scenery. A double green, a 250-foot monster, serves both the 12th and 16th holes.

It took three years to build the course, which opened for play in 1984. More than half a million cubic yards of topsoil were added to the lava base to make Kiahuna's fairways wide and lush.

Interesting remains of old Hawaii have been kept. There are many historic Hawaiian *heiaus* (temples) on the golf course land, in addition to lava tubes, irrigation aqueducts, and the remains of a house believed to have been constructed by the Hawaiians in the early 1800s.

The Poipu area has long been a favorite get-away spot for "locals" — residents of the Aloha State. Its sunny climate and gentle beaches make it fun for the whole family.

Until recently Kiahuna was the sole golfing choice at Poipu. Now, with the opening of the Hyatt Regency Kauai and its adjacent 18 holes, Poipu guests will have two excellent courses to play.

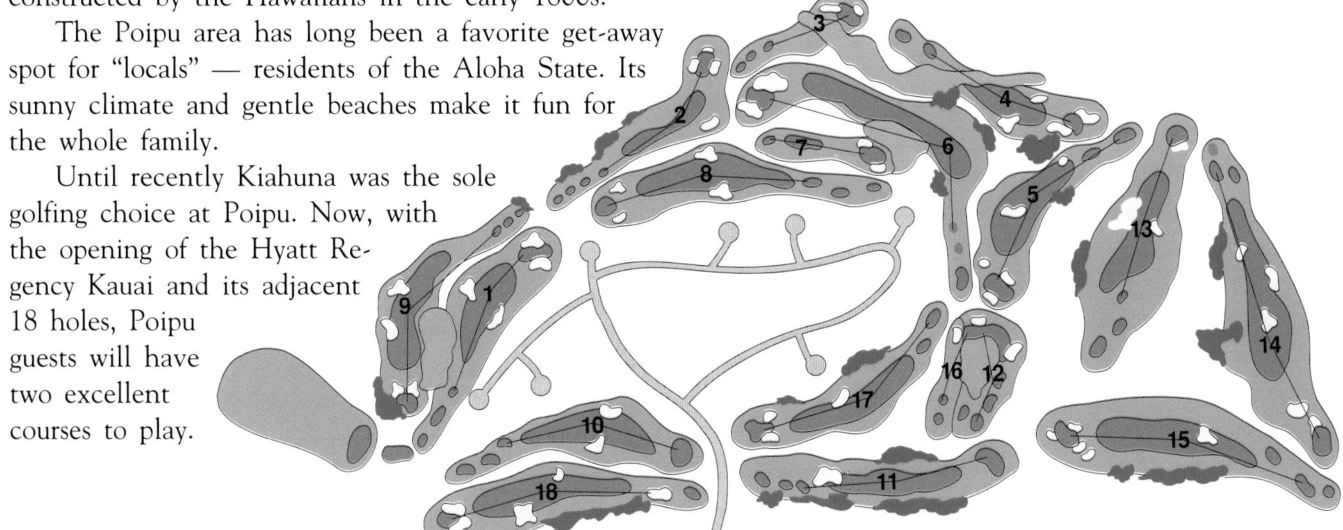

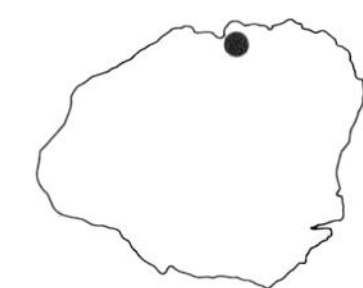

# PRINCEVILLE RESORT
## KAUAI

There are now 45 holes at Princeville with the opening of its crown jewel, The Prince, making it one of Hawaii's biggest golfing complexes.

*(left) Princeville's Ocean course hole 7. Don't let a little thing like shooting over the Pacific Ocean bother you!*

All 45 holes, including the original 27, meander through the incredible coastal scenery of Kauai's northern shore. The ocean cliffs, beaches, and towering, verdant mountains have formed the backdrop for many Hollywood epics, including *South Pacific, Raiders of the Lost Ark, King Kong,* and *The Thorn Birds.*

Princeville is named after the Hawaiian prince, Albert Edward Kauikieouli, the only child of Queen Emma and King Kamehameha IV. Albert was two years old in 1860 when his parents took him for a holiday at the ranch plantation owned by the monarchy's foreign minister, a Scotsman named Robert Crichton Wyllie. Wyllie was so taken by the two-year-old that he named his 11,000-acre plantation Princeville, and suggested the lad be named Baron of Princeville.

Since that grand Victorian era, the majestic setting of the area has become renowned throughout the world, mainly through the Hollywood film makers who discovered Mount Makana, the North Shore's most prominent landmark, some 35 years ago, when they were scouting for the Bali Hai of *South Pacific.*

The original 27-hole layout is comprised of three separate nines: the Ocean, Woods, and Lake. By combining any two of the three nines, a golfer has a 6,900-yard challenge from the back tees, 6,200 from the middle tees, and 5,500 from the women's tees.

Robert Trent Jones, Jr., when he designed the original 27 holes, said, "In all the world, I never expect to find a more spectacularly beautiful place to build a golf course."

The Prince is a delightful new course, which could easily be the best in Hawaii. "The Prince is a great test of golf in its own right, and hard enough to play if you just focus on your game. But the surroundings are so beautiful that keeping focus is going to be difficult," warns Neil Finch, Princeville's director of golf.

He's absolutely right. Trent Jones, Jr. has designed 150 or so courses around the globe, and this is one of his most outstanding examples of golf course architecture.

All in all, Princeville is a special retreat. This distinctive resort is a place to immerse oneself in nature's beauty and rest one's soul!

# PRINCEVILLE MAKAI

## THE OCEAN NINE

*Featured Holes:*

### Hole 7 - 197 Yards Par 3

This hole has often been compared with some of the greatest in golf. The tee is on one side of an ocean inlet, the green on the other, and play from the championship and men's tees carries over the Pacific towards the mystical Bali Hai.

Upcurrents from the 160-foot-deep ocean inlet cause an interesting ball flight pattern. The green here is very large, but not what you'd call easy. The trick is to use enough club to at least reach the other side of the inlet. You can always recover a par from land, never from the depths of the ocean below.

*(below) The afternoon light makes Princeville a special place indeed. Here the Woods course, 5th green.*

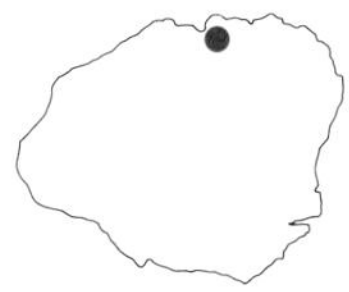

## Hole 9 - 390 Yards Par 4

The Ocean 9th features another wasp-waisted fairway, with three bunkers for a corset. It can be a tough par four, with a dog-leg to the right, into the breeze. To center your drive aim a straight ball at the left-hand fairway bunker and the breeze will position you well for your second shot. It is very important not to become soft here. It is only 160 yards, but it can be a 3-iron from the left bunker. The breeze will slow the ball down and drift it onto the green. Don't go right under any circumstance.

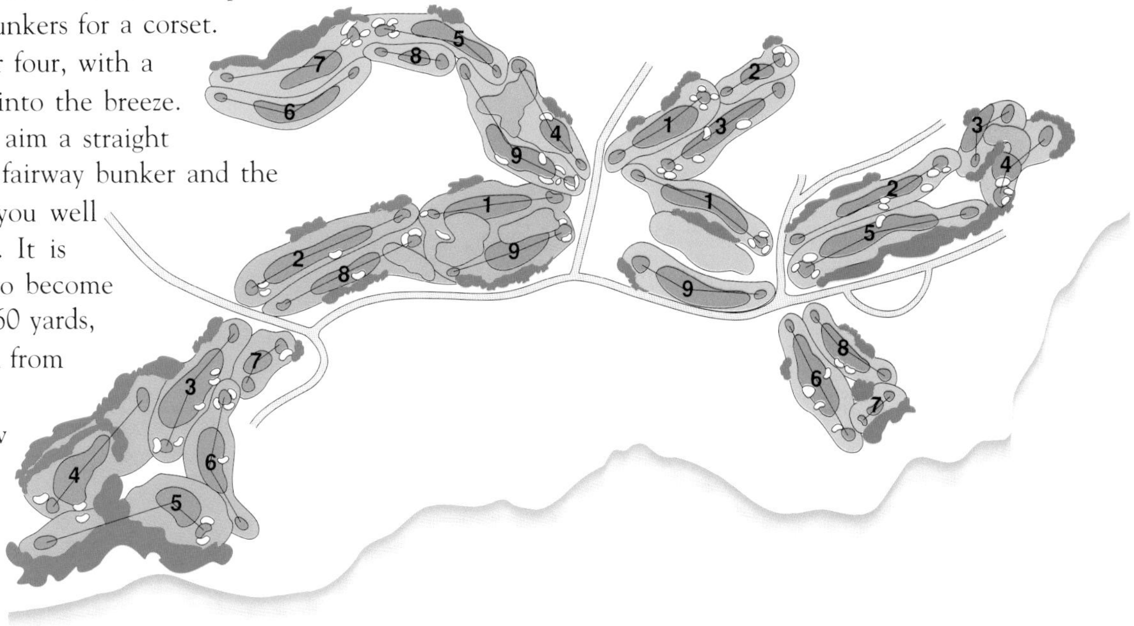

*(above) Princeville Lake course, 7th hole. A par three, 200-yarder.*

## THE LAKE NINE

### Hole 3 - 440 Yards Par 4

The championship tees shoot through trees with a voracious valley to the left of the fairway and bunkering at the one-third and two-thirds points of its left side to trap shots which kick off a sloping fairway. This is the toughest hole on the Lake and it seems a quarter of a mile into the breeze. But make sure you aim your tee shot to the high side of the fairway. The next can be a 3-wood to an elevated triangular green, bunkered on each side of its "chin," which faces the golfer. The wind can also play havoc with the second shot.

### Hole 9 - 510 Yards Par 5

An over-water par five, the championship tees play over a lake to the fairway. Truly a case of whether you "lake it or not." With the following trade-winds, and if you intend to make it in two, fly your driver straight for the African tulip tree or conservatively play your 3-wood to the right of the same tree, carrying a little less lake. If you have been conservative, you cannot make the green with your next shot, so wait for it. Play two consecutive 8-irons: one short of the second lake, the other just to lazily land on the front edge of the small green. Or, if you have let fly for the African tulip, then you have landed on an area large enough to cope with light aircraft, leaving you with a 4- to 5-iron hit quietly to this small green.

*(above) Princeville Woods course, 1st green. A well-bunkered target.*

## THE WOODS COURSE

### Hole 6 - 442 Yards Par 4

This hole is a destroyer, the toughest on the Woods. *"Ke Kokoke mai la ka Mo oilo"* – Beware, lest you shed tears. Forget the fact that this is a dog-leg, certainly at this point. There is no margin for error. A laser-like drive at the hibiscus bush, staying away from a well-placed bunker on the fairway's right, and you will need two wood shots which may still not reach the putting surface. So, mentally prepare yourself that it's a par five. The wind here requires a tactically-tuned shot. Do not concern yourself with the bunker at the back. They say it has never been used.

### Hole 7 - 427 Yards Par 4

This hole's personality is based on the fact that the bend in the dog-leg left is at the early part of the fairway. So it is an invitation to bite off more than you can chew, especially in a cross wind. Usually, however, a tail wind makes this hole a little easier. The next shot presents a bit of a poser if you are going down breeze. You are forced to carry a front bunker and land on a green with the grain running with you. You don't want your ball to have too much momentum when it lands, so hit an 8-iron as high as you can and allow it to just collapse onto the green.

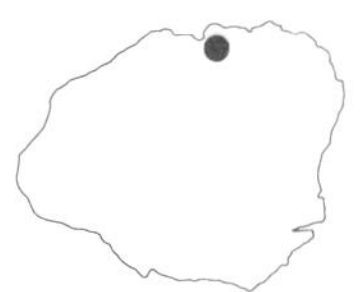

# THE PRINCE
## COURSE

*Featured Holes:*

### Hole 6 - 428 Yards Par 4

This fairway looks like a giant, grassy water chute that the Prince's great-great grandfather, King Kamehameha I, might have had built for himself and family. There is out-of-bounds to the left and the breeze blows in that direction. The clump of trees on the skyline looks like an ideal target. Do not be fooled. It will lead you down the right to a position where you not only can't see the green, but have no indication of where it is. You've lost it! Not even a classified advertisement in the local paper will help you. Fire the driver to the right-hand bunkers and you will finish up in the middle of this gentle swale. Between you and the green is a virtual minefield of bunkers that have to be traversed by means of a well-hit 6-iron. Whatever you do, do not be short, for there is no extreme penalty if you are a little on the long side, except the Pacific, which provides an awe-some backdrop for this hole.

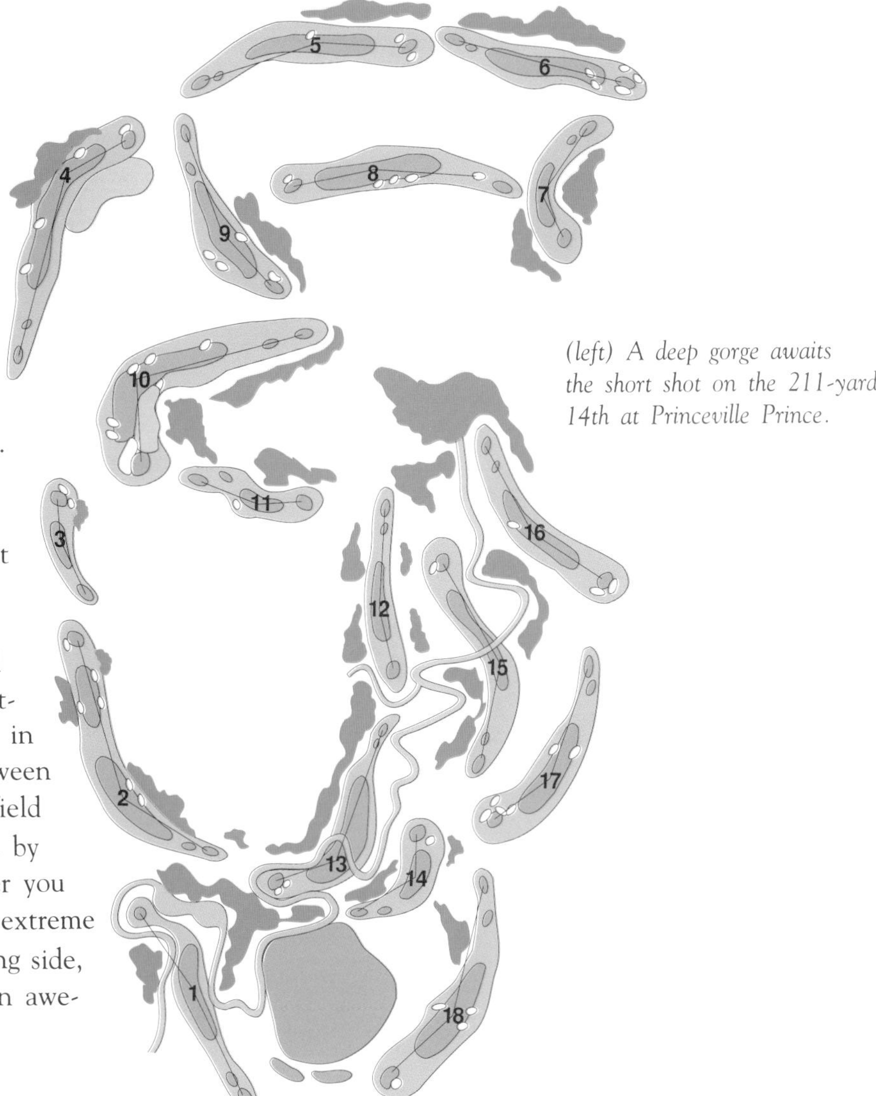


*(left) A deep gorge awaits the short shot on the 211-yard 14th at Princeville Prince.*

*(above) The 4th fairway. Don't drift right.*

## Hole 7 - 205 Yards Par 3

Number 7 is no pussycat—maybe a tiger. It is 205 yards against the tradewinds and carries over a ravine. The championship tee has to carry a ravine that is so deep that the tall trees growing there look like little bushes. The Pacific Ocean on the left, the bright green mountains as a backdrop, and the yawning ravine all combine to take one's breath away. A dash of luck, a smidgin of talent, and a handful of divine assistance should be all you need. Even that might not be enough to make this very large green with your tee shot.

## Hole 12 - 390 Yards Par 4

Referred to as the Eagle's Nest (not because it is easy to score on), this tee is perched 100 feet above the fairway, which looks like a runway cut out of the jungle from up there. Obviously, there is no margin for error on either side, so thump your driver as far down the middle and as low as you can. The ball coming down from such a high tee has virtually no run on it. The distance is in the carry. If you have made good with the drive, you should be only 150 yards away from the green, hopefully with a level stance on the undulating fairway. There is a dense growth surrounding the fairway, and the Anini Stream which wanders every which way, including hugging the back and sides of the green. You are a mid- to short

*(above) The north coast of Kauai often offers spectacular scenery, such as the cloud-covered mountains seen from the 10th tee on the Prince.*

iron away from this split-level green. You need to land on it with a little backspin. So be warned.

## Hole 13 - 418 Yards Par 4

This is another narrow fairway cut through the jungle but bending to the right, the same direction as the prevailing breeze. Do not worry that you cannot see the green and only a small section of the fairway. Aim your tee shot for what little of the fairway that is visible, and hopefully you will position yourself about 175 yards from the green. You are now very much at the business end of the hole. This green is certainly well-guarded. From the plateau where you're standing for your second shot, you can see dark red cliffs. Halfway down these cliffs there emerges a sparkling cascade of water which creates the Anini Stream, which in turn creates most of the problems confronting you. The stream writhes from the left-back of the green down the side, across the front, then down the right side of the fairway and then across the fairway just in front of you—not unlike a giant water python lying in wait. All in all, totally unforgiving. The bunkers at the left are what you aim at with a 4-iron. Don't be worried should you make the bunker; it's preferable to many of the other fates that might befall you. Don't let the beauty of the cascading water sap your concentration dry.

*Danger to the right, danger to the left, danger to the rear. But what a pretty hole the Prince's 13th is!*

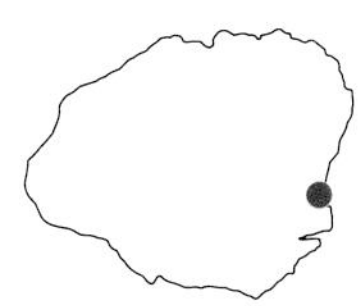

# WAILUA MUNICIPAL
## GOLF COURSE

You will see the Wailua Municipal Golf Course on your right, on the way to Princeville, soon after leaving Lihue airport. Have another look at it, because here is one of the best public course layouts in America.

It is busy. Some 400 rounds a day are played on this honey of a seaside layout, which began its life in 1920 as a three-hole layout. It took another 42 years before it became an 18-hole course.

The player needs to thread his shots through some narrow gaps in the iron-wood trees. These and the rolling fairways and smallish greens make Wailua quite a stern test.

It hosted the U.S.G.A. Men's Public Links Championship in 1975, and *Golf Digest* has named it as one of the best 10 municipal links courses in the country.

If you get through the first holes with a couple of pars you are on the way to a good round. But disappointment can set in early, especially at the 2nd where the wind blows into your face and the narrow fairway is bordered on the left by the pounding surf of the Pacific.

The Wailua area boasts Hawaii's only navigable river, the Wailua River. Its size is attributable to the fact that the Wailua River is recipient of the runoff from what scientists call "the wettest spot on Earth," Mount Waialeale, which receives almost 500 inches of rain per year on its cloud-shrouded peak.

The area is also home to Hawaii's first "fantasy" resort, the Coco Palms, which Elvis Presley popularized with his 1966 film *Blue Hawaii.*

*(left) The 7th green at Wailua, one of the 10 best municipal links courses in the country, according to Golf Digest.*

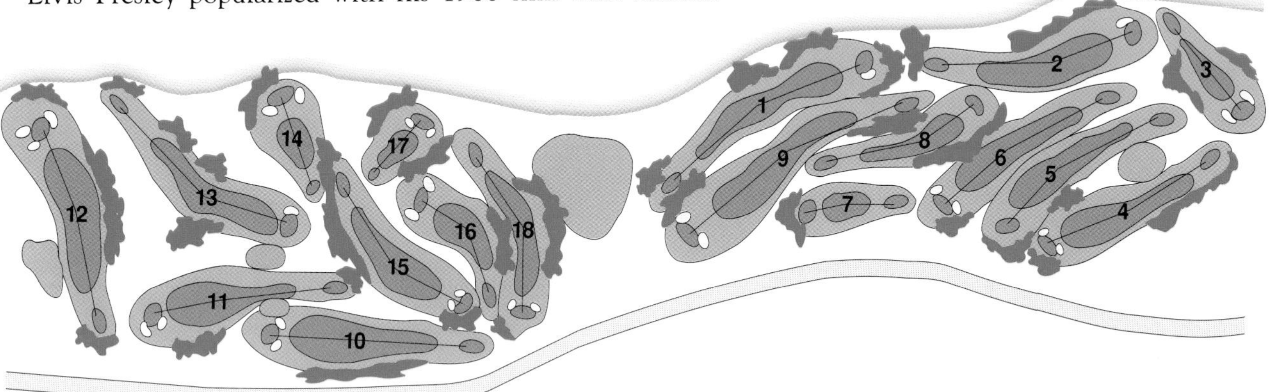

*(above) You don't want to hook your tee shot left on the 2nd at Wailua.*

*Featured Holes:*

## Hole 2 - 456 Yards Par 4

This is the hardest hole on the course. The entire length of the left side of the hole is successfully guarded by the Pacific Ocean. The hole turns a little left and the breeze is from behind. This is an opportunity for you to hit away, with plenty of trust in your driver. Fire left of center and you will make a safe landing in the middle of the "runway." In fact, this hole was the airstrip for a Marine base during World War II. You now have 180 yards to go, so let fly with a 5-iron and pilot the shot towards the left half of the target area.

## Hole 6 - 407 Yards Par 4

This is not baseball, but to master this hole you need to play two consecutive curve balls, both shots bent to the left. Direct your tee shot, played from the left side of the tee, to the right and curve it back to the center. Your second shot, with a 4-iron, aimed at the right green-side bunker should come nicely onto the green.

## Hole 7 - 178 Yards Par 3

This green is very wide at the front then curves in at both sides halfway back. In these two curves there is a bunker, and right across the front there is also a curved bunker. The whole layout looks like a grinning face. But you are going to change that look by hitting a 3-iron right between the eyes and not the expected 5-iron that normally contributes to the Mona Lisa smirk!

*(above) The 11th plays around this quiet little lake.*

## Hole 8 - 403 Yards Par 4

This hole is a cunning one. It dog-legs gradually to the left, and you can see a bunker guarding the left side of the green. The bunker is out of range, but don't stay left. What you don't see are the trees on the left guarding not only the left green but also the bunker. There is just no way in. So fire your driver to the bunker but have it come back to the right. Then you should have a comfortable but firm 5-iron also coming in from the left.

## Hole 14 - 168 Yards Par 3

An elevated tee, an elevated green, with a swale in between. The back of this generous green has a collar of ironwood trees, and that is all that separates the green from the Pacific Ocean, the source of the prevailing tradewinds, so club selection is very important. The breeze will add 20 yards to the hole, so select the appropriate club. Then all that is left is to hit the ball absolutely straight, directly at the center of the green.

## Hole 18 - 394 Yards Par 4

Don't believe what you see on this finishing hole. From the elevated tee, it seems all you have to do is bend your driver from left to right around the bend. Well, that is dangerous. Instead, still using your driver, hit the ball left of center and let Mother Nature bend it to the right for you. This is much more practical and less damaging to your score. Now for a self-satisfying shot, with aggression, punish an 8-iron from 150 yards out onto this green, using the wind. Two putts later, you have completed one of the top municipal courses in the United States.

ISLAND OF

# OAHU

The island of Oahu is home to 800,000 of the state's population of one million people. It is also recipient of more than 80 percent of Hawaii's six million visitors each year, the majority of whom frequent the hotels of Waikiki. No wonder the island is called the Gathering Place.

But Oahu is much more than just Waikiki. In fact, the business community of Honolulu is a fast-paced center of international commerce. In recent years, Honolulu has more and more become known as "the hub of the Pacific," with strong links to Tokyo, Hong Kong, Singapore — all of Asia.

On the North Shore, some of the best surfing in the world is to be found at Sunset Beach, Waimea, and the Banzai Pipeline. Up the road at Mokuleia, the Hawaii Polo Club performs against a backdrop of rolling blue surf and jade green mountains. On the south shore, world-famous Hanauma Bay gives visitors to Oahu a gentle glimpse of the colorful undersea life found in Hawaii.

All of this, combined with a favorable year-round climate, adds up to an exciting vacation experience which is not easily matched.

*Waikiki Beach with Diamond Head, Hawaii's most recognizable landmark, proudly standing in the background.*

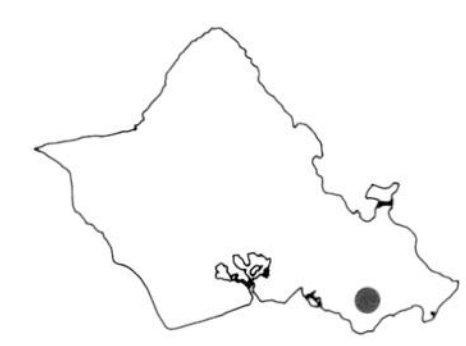

# ALA WAI
## MUNICIPAL GOLF COURSE

The Ala Wai Municipal Golf Course, behind the Waikiki tourist strip, is on some of the most valuable land in Honolulu. It was the first public golf course on the island of Oahu.

It is also the busiest golf course in the world. According to the *Guinness Book of World Records*, Ala Wai caters to 500 rounds daily, or around 180,000 a year, the first players hitting off just before dawn, the last putting out with car headlights switched on to give them a look at the flagstick.

The popularity of the layout, of course, is attributed to its centralized location, reasonable fees, and the relatively rain free climate of Honolulu.

As an added convenience, Ala Wai has a "dial-a-time" system, whereby players can obtain starting times one week in advance by calling on the phone.

There is not a lot of trouble to stop golfers playing quickly. The wind, however, occasionally causes problems with club selection.

*(left) The 1st fairway on the world's busiest golf course, Ala Wai, right behind the Waikiki tourist strip.*

*Featured Holes:*

### Hole 2 - 208 Yards Par 3

This hole is made honest by the prevailing breeze, which influences your shot from left to right. Your tee shot needs to hold into the strong trades as the green slopes left to right. A reservoir waits for you, both to the right and back of the green, so don't be too aggressive.

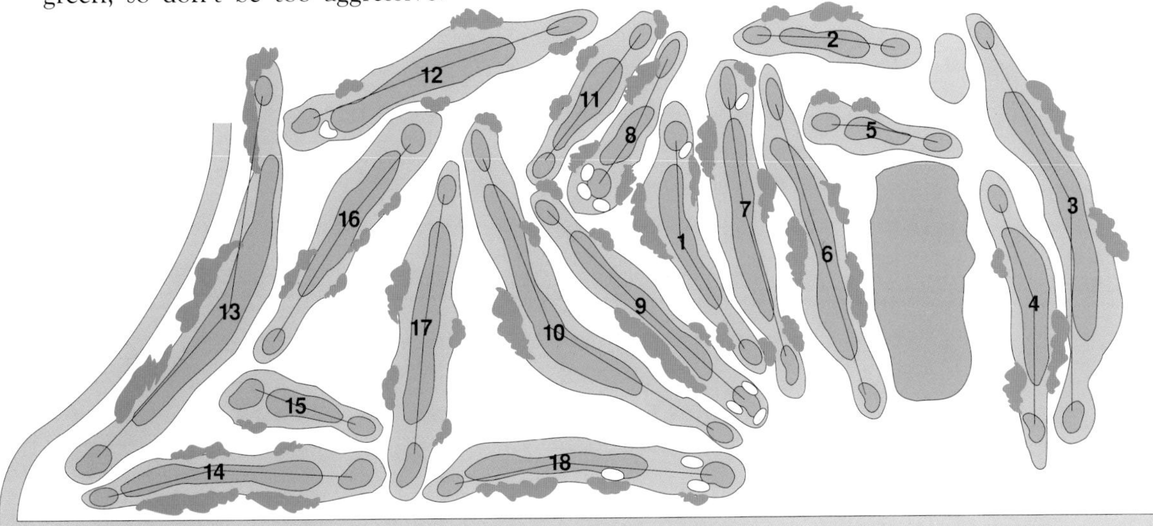

*(above) The 7th green offers golfers a slightly different view of Diamond Head.*

## Hole 4 - 356 Yards Par 4

While on the subject of honesty, this hole is another typical example. You are driving into the teeth of the trades. There are ironwood trees both right and left and a fairway bunker waiting for you on the left. So drive just past the bunker on its left side. All you should need then is a well-punched 8-iron onto the green, dissecting the green-side bunker. Try to finish on the same level as the pin.

## Hole 11 - 186 Yards Par 3

Don't let the yardage on this one-shot hole fool you. Mentally add another 20 yards and select your club accordingly. This green looks innocent enough, but don't be fooled by that either. If you miss this green, right or left, you can too easily turn this hole into a par four.

## Hole 16 - 324 Yards Par 4

This hole drives into the teeth of the wind. On the right there is a bunker and two monkeypod trees—try to keep away from them. The pear-shaped green,

*(above) A view from Waikiki shows the number of trees which protect Ala Wai's greens.*

in the company of a left-hand bunker and right-hand mound, plays a little further than you would think, so add an extra club and punch it low and hard.

## Hole 17 - 360 Yards Par 4

A local man-made landmark guards the left side of this fairway—it's called Kobayashi Mountain. Make the decision to keep to the center, it's more sensible. Now remember, with the wind behind you, don't get too excited and overclub. The green itself doesn't present any real problem if you keep clear of the bunkers and mounds.

## Hole 18 - 360 Yards Par 4

A good finishing hole. To keep your drive honest, there's the man-made Kobayashi Mountain on the left and the Ala Wai Canal running down the right side. There is also a bunker 220 yards out. Add to all this a cluster of Samoan palms on the right, coconut palms to the left, and just to complete this busy picture, as a backdrop there is the famous Diamond Head. Your approach shot needs to bisect the green-side bunkers, after carrying a devilishly placed burn.

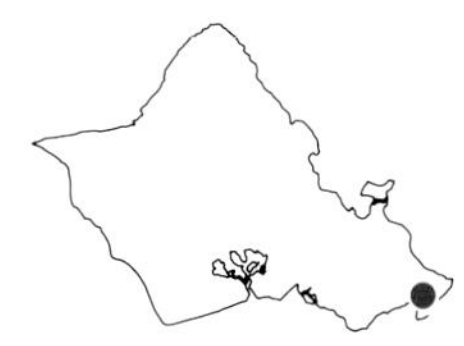

# HAWAII KAI
## GOLF COURSE

The Hawaii Kai course is located some 15 miles east of Waikiki, and there is some spectacular coastline and interesting scenery along the way.

The championship course, kept busy by visitors to Waikiki, is another Billy Bell design. It is 6,686 yards long, a par 72, which overlooks the ocean and a couple of surfing beaches close by.

It is well-maintained, despite its 90,000 annual rounds, and is not terribly difficult, with a sense of freedom prevailing in its uncluttered design—although water and sand do make a few holes quite challenging and the tradewinds constantly keep you alert.

A fascinating addition to the flora here is the milo or "message tree." It is seen all over the course, thriving on sandy soil and the salt spray from the nearby surf. It produces a wide, leather-like leaf, and on these leaves, using a golf tee, players scrawl messages which can still be read five years later. It all makes for interesting reading if your game is off target.

*(left) This shot is taken from the 5th tee box at Hawaii Kai, and shows that golfers must shoot over a small swale to an open green.*

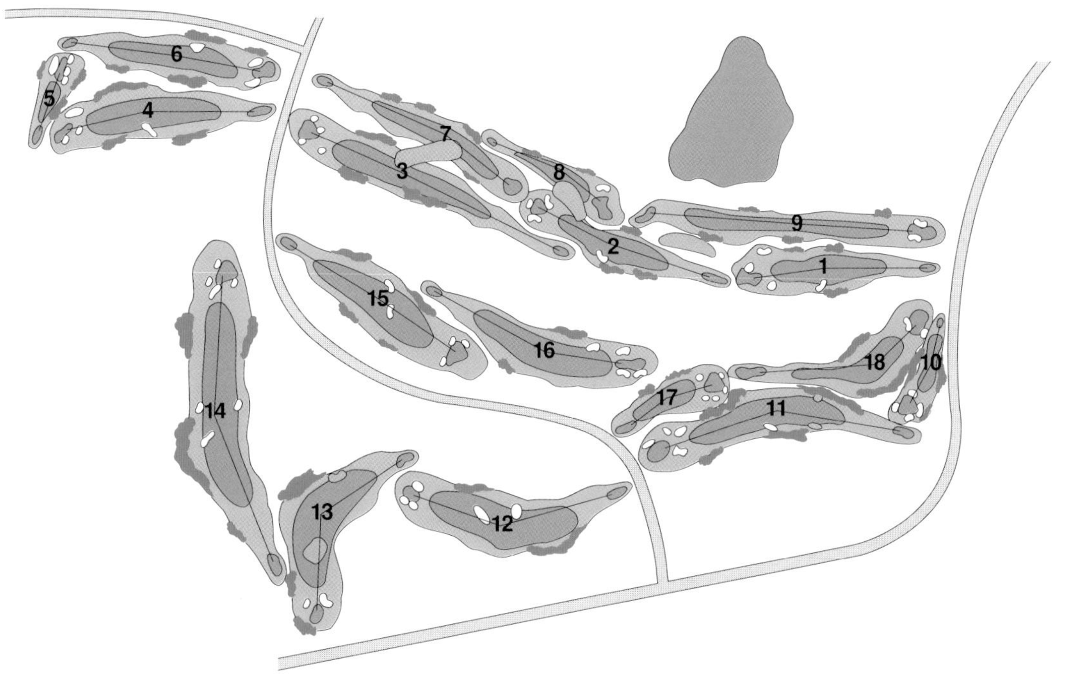

*(above) Koko Crater provides the backdrop for Hawaii Kai's 8th green.*

*Featured Holes:*

## Hole 3 - 517 Yards Par 5

This is a tight driving hole made so by two trees just 50 yards from the elevated tee and only 40 yards apart. Don't go right, unless you are fond of water, or left, unless you want to visit a friend living in one of the homes bordering the out-of-bounds. This 517-yard par five hole can be reached in two, but be careful. The green, while being very wide, is not so deep. A following breeze, plus an elevated green, plus lack of depth could spell trouble. The alternative is to lay-up short with a long iron or 3-wood, leaving virtually a "kick on" wedge for your third shot. At this stage a four is still possible, certainly a five is assured.

## Hole 7 - 399 Yards Par 4

Before you drive this short par four, think. If you use your driver perfectly, you will be in the narrowest part of the fairway with water on the right and out-of-bounds on the left, leaving you a neck of only 30 paces in between. If you mis-hit, though, you're in trouble. So play your tee shot with a long iron short, but safe. This should leave you with a 170-yard second shot over an outreach of water to a green that slopes from six feet at the back to zero in the front. As well, you are playing into the breeze. If you learned anything on the previous green, please remember it. This green is more so. *I ka nana no a ike*—by observing one learns.

*(above) The 2nd fairway asks you to avoid the pleasures of sandtraps such as this one.*

## Hole 8 - 207 Yards Par 3

Here is an honest hole, 207 yards from an elevated tee to an elevated green. You should be into the breeze, with a reservoir on your right. This requires you to punish a long iron onto the well-bunkered green. The backdrop to this target is quite distracting — a 60-foot-high mound absolutely ablaze with color, then the white capped waves in-between you and the Friendly Isle — Molokai. So keep your head down and concentrate.

## Hole 10 - 170 Yards Par 3

Select your normal club for a 170-yard shot. Put it back in the bag and take two clubs less. Forget the bunkers, the green is not only big, but has plenty of definition.

## Hole 13 - 427 Yards Par 4

A severe dog-leg left makes for a wise choice of a 4-wood from the tee. Aim for the 150-yard hibiscus marker, which should place your ball in the center of the bend and the fairway. If you happen to duff your tee shot, make sure your profanity is inaudible, as the tee is only 11 paces from somebody's front door. At 150 yards from the green, the breeze is coming over your left shoulder, so club selection is based purely on the force of the tradewind. Do not attempt to short-cut this hole, as there is a monstrous water hazard on the left.

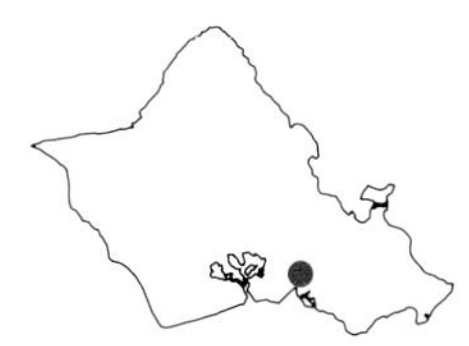

# HONOLULU
## COUNTRY CLUB

*(left) A 512-yard par five beauty, the 18th at Honolulu Country Club.*

This very private club in Honolulu is attractively carved out of former swampland and offers quite a demanding test of the game.

Water makes the 6,801-yard course quite challenging, and this most penalizing hazard of the game is particularly evident over the final six holes. On this stretch, water either borders, separates, or protects the greens and fairways.

The course was designed by Francis Duane with input from Arnold Palmer, opening for play in 1977. Distances from the tees can be gauged by reflector discs on the cart paths. Membership is limited to 500 at Honolulu Country Club, making it one of the more exclusive clubs in Hawaii.

*Featured Holes:*

### Hole 2 - 508 Yards Par 5

This par five can be reached in two if you put plenty of power in your drive. The wind is over your left shoulder and the fairway dog-legs left, so force your drive to veer slightly left of center. The emphasis is on "slightly," as the water hazard on the left also snakes around the back of the green. You now have a full 3-wood shot, hitting out of a gentle swale, which gives the impression that the green is elevated.

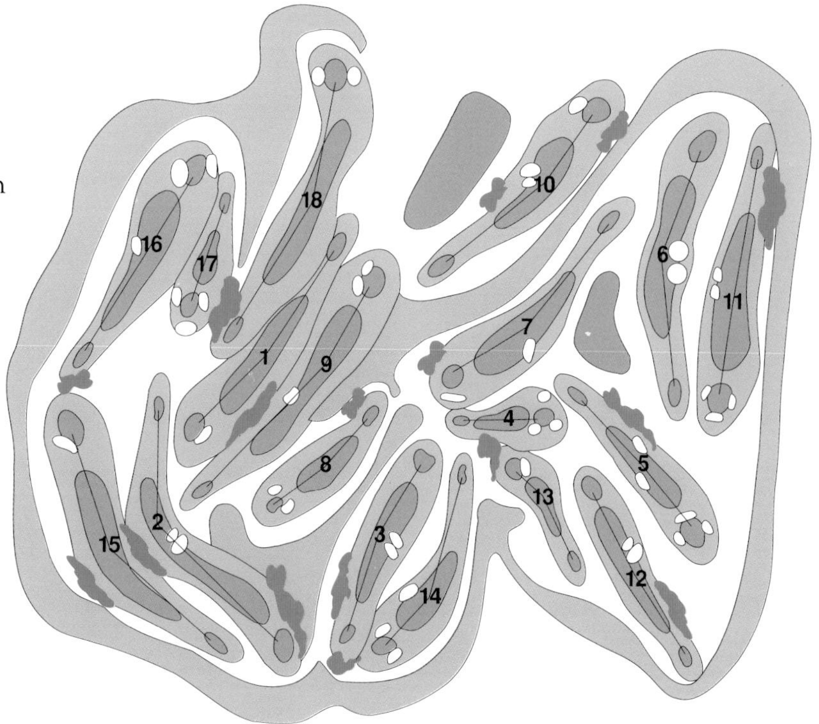

*(above) Blue skies and abundant water set off nearly every hole at Honolulu Country Club, as is evident here at the 13th.*

## Hole 6 - 453 Yards Par 4

This is the hardest hole on the course. Because of the holding power of the prevailing tradewinds, add another 30 yards to this hole. Your nerve could be really tested on this one. There is out-of-bounds on both sides of the fairway, so keep your head down and give it all you've got with your driver.

## Hole 7 - 402 Yards Par 4

With a bunker encroaching onto the left side of this fairway 190 yards from the tee, you can spinnaker this drive and let the wind do all the work. A water hazard runs the whole length of the right side and then curls gently around the back of the green. You now need a 9-iron to cover the remaining 135 yards to the green, which sits a little higher than your stance.

## Hole 13 - 197 Yards Par 3

This hole is somewhat overwhelming. Consider these facts: water from left to right, tradewinds from right to left, big yawning bunkers on both sides of the

*(above) The 6th green is bordered by highrises in the Salt Lake area of Honolulu.*

green, a green you cannot see due to the bougainvillea, and if that's not enough, the green slopes down from front to back. Take what you need and hit the ball 197 yards, after you have computed the wind conditions.

## Hole 18 - 512 Yards Par 5

The yardage on this hole indicates you may make the green in two shots. This is not so when you take into consideration that the tradewinds add a possible 30 to 40 yards to the distance of this hole. Down the left side of this fairway is water. Lining the right side is a row of palm trees. So it is time to draw upon your last remnants of energy and aim your tee shot right of center and have the wind float it gently back to the middle. This hole has a gentle, almost crescent-like curve to the left. For the adventurous, there is an invitation to carry some water and try to make this green in two. If you prefer not to take the chance and spoil a good card, just lay-up with a 5-iron and pancake a wedge onto the green.

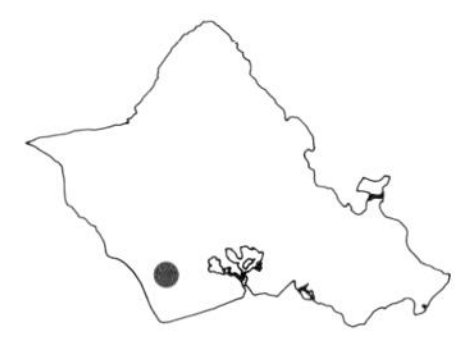

# KO OLINA
## GOLF CLUB

Ko Olina is the newest golf resort on the island of Oahu. It is located west of Honolulu, near the Barbers Point Naval Air Station, on the southwest tip of the island.

Designed by Ted Robinson, the course at Ko Olina opened in early 1990 as the first phase of an ambitious development project. In addition to the 6,867-yard golf layout, plans for Ko Olina include several top-notch hotels, a marina, a shopping center, and some condominiums.

Robinson, who with golfing great Greg Norman also designed a new course on the island of Lanai called the Experience at Koele, took a flat, dusty Ko Olina landscape and transformed it into gently rolling hills and valleys, bordered by plenty of water. In fact, it is fair to say that the water features define the personality of the course. On several holes Robinson didn't simply insert ponds and lakes, but instead designed a beautiful series of stepped brooks and bubbling waterfalls.

For an accomplished player, though, the water will only come into play on four holes, with the par three 8th and 12th holes probably the most picturesque. On the 8th, you shoot from an elevated tee to a split-level elevated green which is coyly resting behind a three-tiered waterfall and a lush bed of bougainvillea.

Overall Ko Olina is not a terribly difficult course to play, yet it will provide a thoughtful challenge. The 150-yard markers are colorful sprays of bougainvillea. And the scorecard warns, "The Ko Olina 'keep pace program' of 15 minutes per hole will be closely monitored." So enjoy the scenery, but don't lag!

*(left) The 12th tee of Ko Olina, Oahu's newest golf resort. This promises to be among the most photographed holes in the state.*

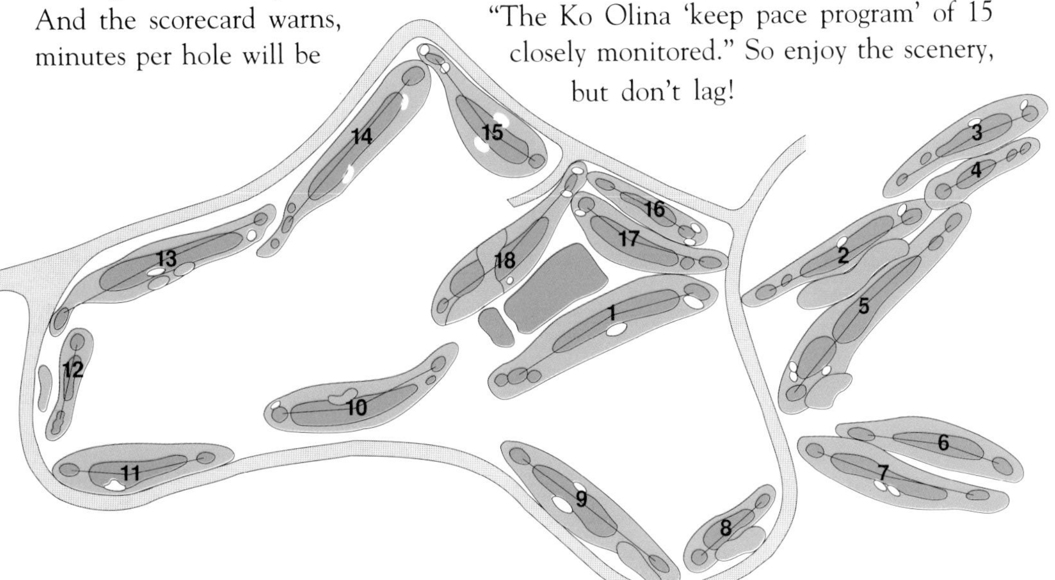

*Typical Ko Olina: rolling fairways and well-guarded greens. Here a view of the 15th hole.*

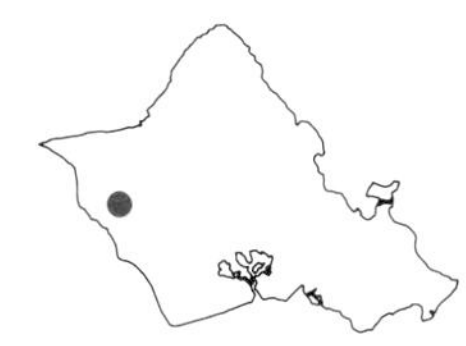

# SHERATON MAKAHA
## RESORT AND COUNTRY CLUB

*(left) With a row of apartments set into the Waianae cliffs as a backdrop, the 10th green at Sheraton Makaha.*

Waianae is a district of bold cliffs and a beautiful sea, 30 miles towards the sunset from Honolulu.

Here, two massive mountains form a deep, green valley which opens to the ocean. It is known as Makaha Valley and it is the site of two golf courses. Soaring Mount Kaala, at 5,000 feet, is visible from every part of both courses.

Developer Chinn Ho first announced plans to develop this valley as a resort in the mid-1960s. His initial plans included using helicopters and hydrofoils to transport visitors from Waikiki.

He also envisioned Makaha as the next big resort center. Fortunately, the Waianae district remains much the same as it was 30 years ago, hardly touched by the commercial world.

In May, 1967, shortly before Chinn Ho broke ground for his hotel and golf courses, both designed by William Bell, police raided a cockfight on a property on Kaakea Road in Waianae Valley, arresting 574 men and women.

This raid firmly established Waianae as the cockfight capital of Hawaii. The reputation still lingers today, although nearby Makaha Beach is perhaps better known by those who seek to pit their bodies against some of the world's most violently surging surf.

The two courses, the Sheraton Makaha Resort course and the Makaha Valley course, are vastly different in terms of difficulty. The resort course, at 7,091 yards, can destroy your game if the wind blows. From the championship tees, it is a thoroughly searching examination of the game, and its reputation as a tough, but fair layout comes from its eight water hazards and 107 bunkers, with the wind often making certain you have everything you could hope for in the way of a challenge.

The scenery is a visual feast. The opening nine meanders down toward the ocean before heading up into the valley, with rugged mountain walls on both sides.

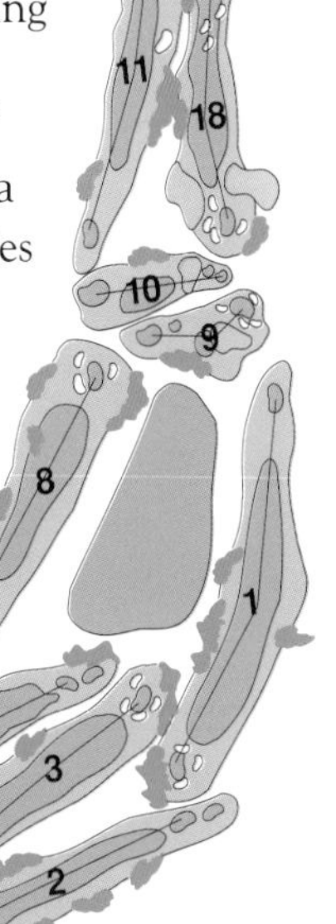

*(above) The par four, 421-yard 2nd hole at Sheraton Makaha.*

Featured Holes:

## Hole 1 - 550 Yards Par 5

A good opening hole. Even with full assistance of the trades, it's still not easy. At 350 yards, in the center of the fairway, is a kiawe tree with branches outstretched right and left — a scarecrow keeping away the birdies. The sensible drive is either left or right of center. Follow this with a 3-wood with a slight left-to-right influence into the gentle swale in front of the green. Then, throw a half-wedge up onto the green, keeping below the pin as the grain runs uphill.

## Hole 5 - 460 Yards Par 5

The hardest hole on the course, there is out-of-bounds along the left side, all the way to the back of the green. The 5th is a dog-leg right, so aim at the left side of the second bunker right of center, as the breeze will nurse it back into the center of the fairway. Hidden 85 yards from the tee is a water hazard which should not come into play. The fairway is undulating and can confuse club selection. If you see a 6-iron, put it back and take a 4-iron. The tradewinds pick up velocity at the bend of the dog-leg, which warrants this change of club.

*(above) A line of coconut palms protects the 5th fairway. A mis-hit tee shot will land you in a difficult lie.*

## Hole 8 - 430 Yards Par 4

With out-of-bounds on the left and a creek in front of the elevated tee, the 8th is a straight-away hole with the fairway sloping right to left. The breeze, however, is the opposite, and there is plenty of rough country along the right-hand side. Drive at the right edge of the green-side bunker, which should leave you with a 150-yard second shot to the elevated green. If you think it's a 6-iron, take a 5. Always allow an extra club for an uphill shot. Note the left-hand bunker has a high back collar.

## Hole 12 - 498 Yards Par 5

This dog-leg par five has out-of-bounds on the left and also at the back of the green. Your tee shot will usually be into a head wind, so aim for the palm-topped mound on the right side of the fairway. A 3-wood second shot is played from one plateau down to another plateau, a drop of some 60 feet, to an unseen green. Play this shot left of center, away from the water hazard. You should then find yourself in perfect position for a wedge onto the putting surface. This is a hole where strategy pays. Don't gamble.

*The Makaha area in rural Oahu is not on the beaten path. But golfers who find their way here will find it a pleasant surprise. Here the 18th on the Sheraton resort course.*

# MAKAHA VALLEY
## COUNTRY CLUB

The Makaha Valley Country Club, like the Sheraton course next door, is flanked by the Makaha-Keeau ridge on one side, and the Makaha-Waianae ridge on the other. From the highest point of the course, the views are often dramatic and breathtaking as you gaze out upon the Pacific Ocean. Of course, the farther up the valley you go, the more likely the chance of rain.

The Makaha Valley course measures 6,369 yards from the championship tees, offering a not-so-nerve-wracking test of one's abilities. However, there are many fairway water hazards and bunkers to keep you on your toes, and the greens are undulating, requiring careful study.

As on most courses in Hawaii, wind is a factor in your play, perhaps more so on the Makaha courses because of their placement at the mouth of the valley. Clearly, this will affect your club selection, and if the wind is whipping, will affect your final score, too.

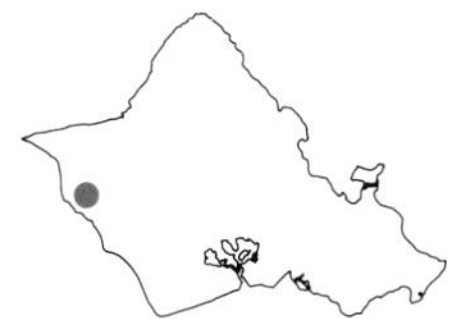

This course offers many interesting holes. The 10th, for instance, a 485-yard par five, is lengthened by the fact that it's uphill, into the wind all the way. To add to the challenge, the green is elevated, and therefore not visible. And there are yawning bunkers right front and right rear.

The ending five holes must be treated with respect and aggression simultaneously — a par three, three par fours, and a par five on the 18th. The trees, the sloping of the fairways and greens, and the varying winds make this sequence of holes quite interesting, indeed.

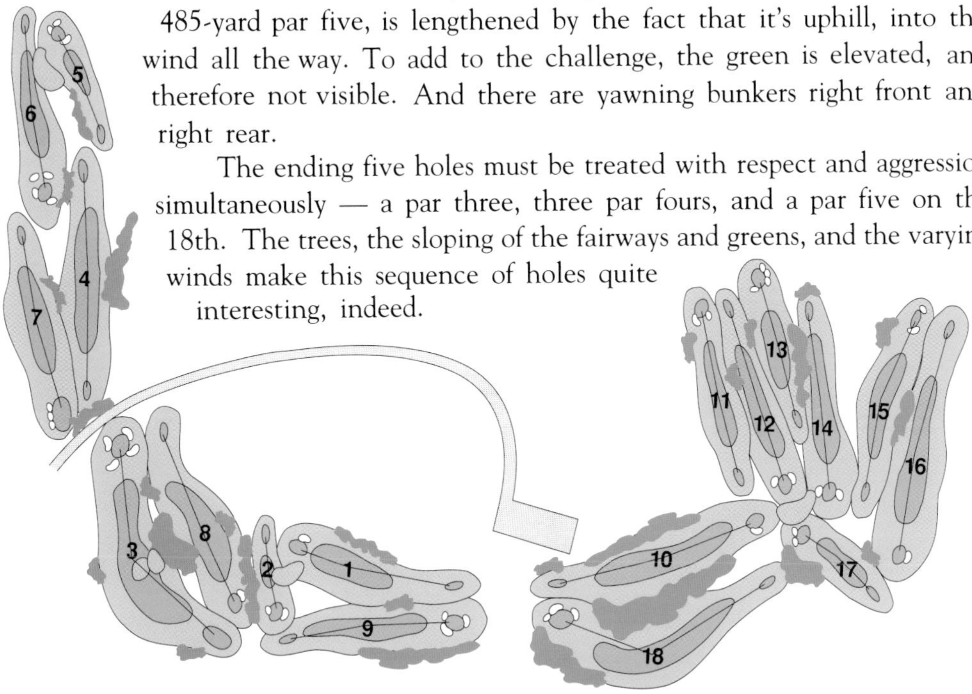

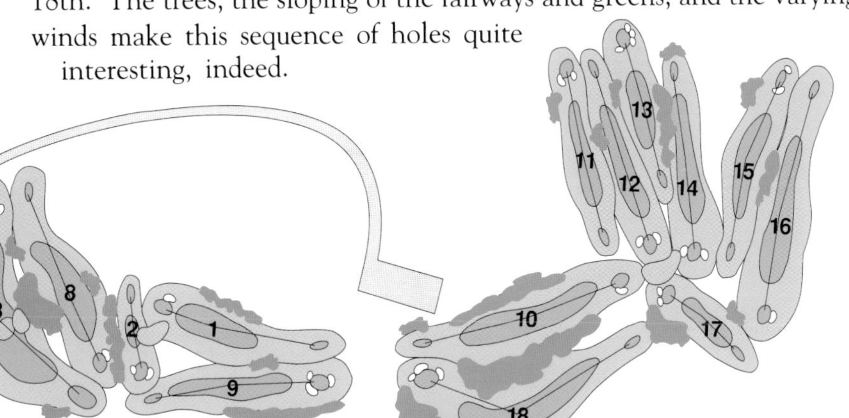


*(below) The Makaha Valley course is buttressed by the Waianae mountains, as is evident in this shot of the 10th fairway.*

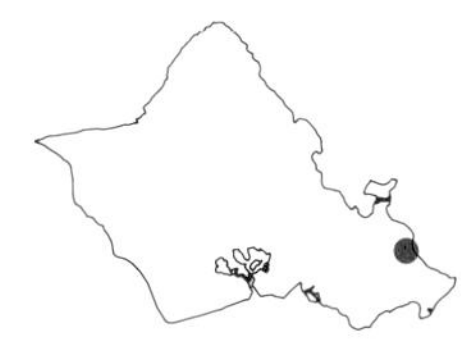

# MID-PACIFIC
## COUNTRY CLUB

*(left) Located in Lanikai, on Oahu's windward side, Mid-Pacific offers golfers a moderate challenge and great views of the Koolau mountains.*

Mid-Pacific Country Club is a private, 600-member club located on the windward side of Oahu. It is near the residential and resort community of Lanikai, which boasts one of the most beautiful and serene white sand beaches in Hawaii. Just offshore of Lanikai Beach are the twin islands known as the Mokuluas. With its gentle tradewinds and abundance of swaying palms, Lanikai is an area which prompts visitors to make comments such as, "This is exactly what I thought Hawaii would be like." It's often that way for residents, too!

The club is different from other private clubs on Oahu in that non-members can play the course during "non-restricted" times: Wednesday, Thursday, and Friday before 11:30 a.m. On the other hand, you'd *really* have to want to play Mid-Pac because the fee for non-members is a whopping $150.00.

One of the most interesting holes on the course must be the 5th. It is a par five, 517-yard dog-leg left, which is bordered all along the right by a tributary from nearby Enchanted Lakes. The green for the hole is on a little island in the tributary, measuring a slim 39 yards across, requiring a short water carry to reach it. The trick is your second shot: using a mid- to long iron, depending on the force of the crosswind, better players can make the green in two. But before you start thinking eagle, make sure your ball lands on the green, instead of in the all-too-inviting water.

At 6,509 yards from the middle tees, Mid-Pacific is one of the longest courses in the state. It ambles over 163 acres of land, featuring a long and generally flat front nine. The back nine, though, is built on the lower slopes of a mountain, which is most evident as you head for the clubhouse on the last five holes. To add to the challenge of the course, the finishing holes are also playing into the wind.

Here's a tip: when you're done with your round of golf on this interesting, and at times difficult course, head on over to Buzz's Lanikai Steak House for a round of mai tais and a dig into their fabulous salad bar. It's just down the street.

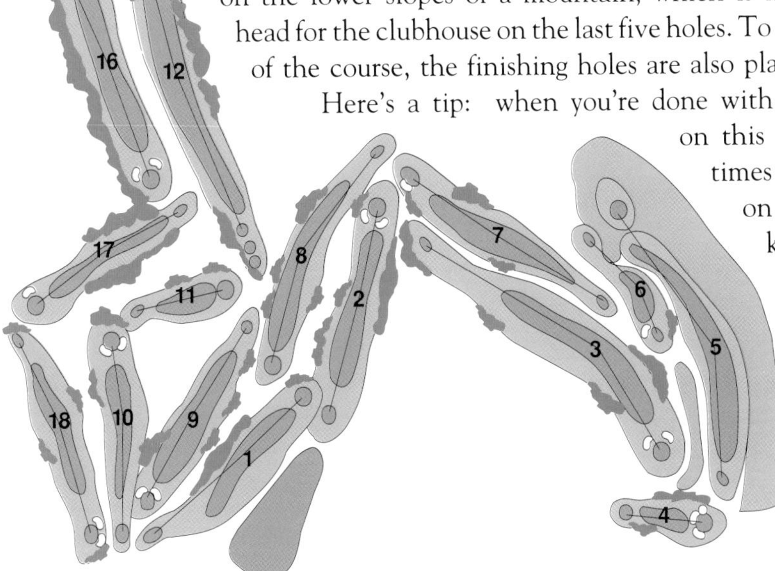

# MILILANI
## GOLF COURSE

The majority of Hawaii's golf courses are built seaside, often boasting panoramic views of the Pacific Ocean on at least a few of their holes. On Oahu, though, several courses nestle against the towering Koolau and Waianae mountain ranges, providing a much different atmosphere for golf. The Mililani Golf Course is one such layout, sitting between those two ranges on central Oahu's Leilehua Plateau.

Since 1967, when it first opened for play, Mililani Golf Course has been one of the most popular layouts on Oahu, particularly among residents. Although the course is relatively flat and usually unaffected by Hawaii's strong winds, it presents the golfer with several design challenges.

Its 18 holes most often utilize traditional bunkering right and left front of the greens, with a few holes—notably 1, 10, 17, and 18—bunkered devilishly just at the bend of their dog-legs. Course hazards also include natural streams and ponds, as well as the man-made Waiahole Ditch—feeding the sugarcane fields of the Oahu Sugar Company—which cuts through the front nine.

*(below) Mililani is an inland course, with fabulous mountain views. Here, on the par three 16th, golfers must avoid a little fairway swim to retrieve an errant shot.*

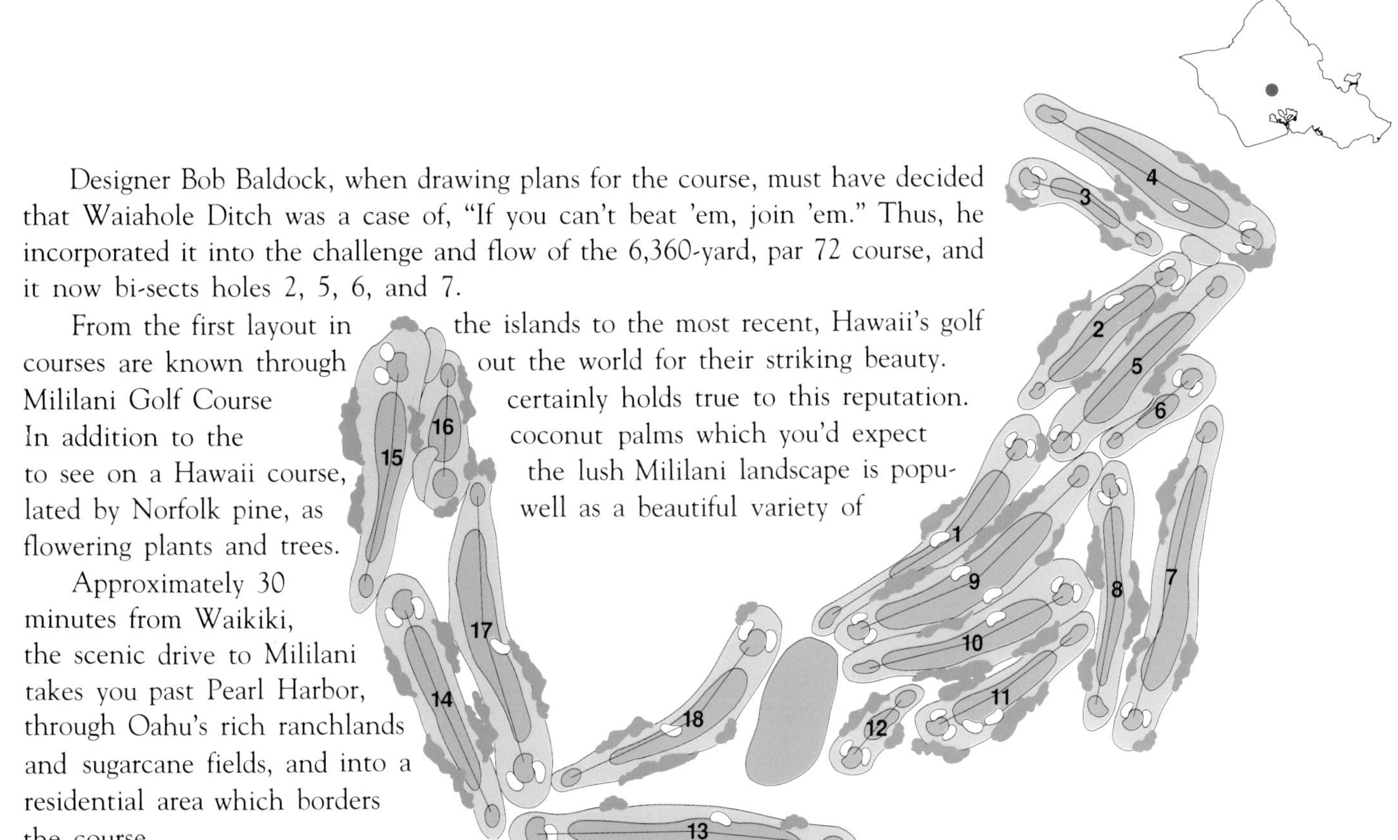


Designer Bob Baldock, when drawing plans for the course, must have decided that Waiahole Ditch was a case of, "If you can't beat 'em, join 'em." Thus, he incorporated it into the challenge and flow of the 6,360-yard, par 72 course, and it now bi-sects holes 2, 5, 6, and 7.

From the first layout in the islands to the most recent, Hawaii's golf courses are known throughout the world for their striking beauty. Mililani Golf Course certainly holds true to this reputation. In addition to the coconut palms which you'd expect to see on a Hawaii course, the lush Mililani landscape is populated by Norfolk pine, as well as a beautiful variety of flowering plants and trees.

Approximately 30 minutes from Waikiki, the scenic drive to Mililani takes you past Pearl Harbor, through Oahu's rich ranchlands and sugarcane fields, and into a residential area which borders the course.

# MILITARY COURSES

There are nine military courses on Oahu, with three of them being nine-hole courses. Only one is a par three course, appropriately named Hickam Par 3 Golf Course. It is, however, very close to the Hickam Malama Bay Golf Course, a full 18-hole, par 72 layout, designed by Bob Baldock. Both courses are located on the grounds of Hickam Air Force base, which air passengers will notice as they are on final approach to Honolulu International Airport.

Probably the three most challenging of the military courses in the state are the Navy-Marine Golf Course and the Kaneohe Klipper Golf Course—both designed by Billy Bell—and Leilehua Golf Course, whose design heritage seems to be a mystery. Most agree that Army engineers and local golfers were responsible for the course layout, although some insist that Willard G. Wilkinson was the designer.

*(below) The Navy-Marine course is one of Hawaii's most scenic military courses. Here a group of golfers putts out on the 17th.*

Regardless, the Leilehua course, located at Schofield Barracks' East Range Training Area, offers 6,521 yards of testing golf. The back nine is particularly tricky, as the fairways narrow and the bunkering becomes more protective of the greens.

More picturesque, if somewhat less demanding, are the Navy-Marine course and the Kaneohe Klipper course. The Navy-Marine course, also located near the Honolulu airport, opened in 1948. It measures 6,758 yards, and the fairways replaced what was called "Tent City" during World War II, after the conglomeration of temporary shelter the area held during military operations in the Pacific.

On the windward side of the island, the Kaneohe Klipper course is built at the Kaneohe Marine Corps Air Station. It is a course which features spectacular scenery, as well as areas of historic note. The sand dunes fronting holes 13 and 14 as they run along the ocean are sacred ground to the Hawaiian people, as they were used for burial grounds in ancient times.

The course itself is relatively flat, but it is subject to strong winds. This, as it does on many Hawaii courses, can make for extremely lively play.

Other military courses on Oahu are Barber's Point, Fort Shafter, Kalakaua, and Ford Island.

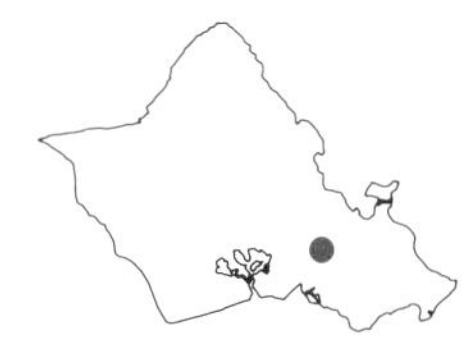

# OAHU
## COUNTRY CLUB

Oahu Country Club, with its breathtaking view of downtown Honolulu and the Pacific Ocean beyond, is situated in the Nuuanu Valley, with the Pali Highway and its surrounding mountain range forming a spectacular boundary.

It is the second oldest club in Hawaii (the oldest being Moanalua, built in 1898), and was first built in 1905 in the Manoa Valley. It moved to its present location in 1907.

It is a private club, home of the Manoa Cup, or Hawaii State Amateur Championship. Visitors, used to larger, modern greens on the newer resort courses, often find themselves at odds with the small greens with slick putting surfaces.

Economic use has been made of the creeks that border some fairways, and these too pose a challenge on the shortish, 5,942-yard, par 71 layout.

*(left) Oahu Country Club is situated in the hills surrounding the Pali Highway. Many holes are high enough to offer great views of downtown Honolulu, such as here on the 11th.*

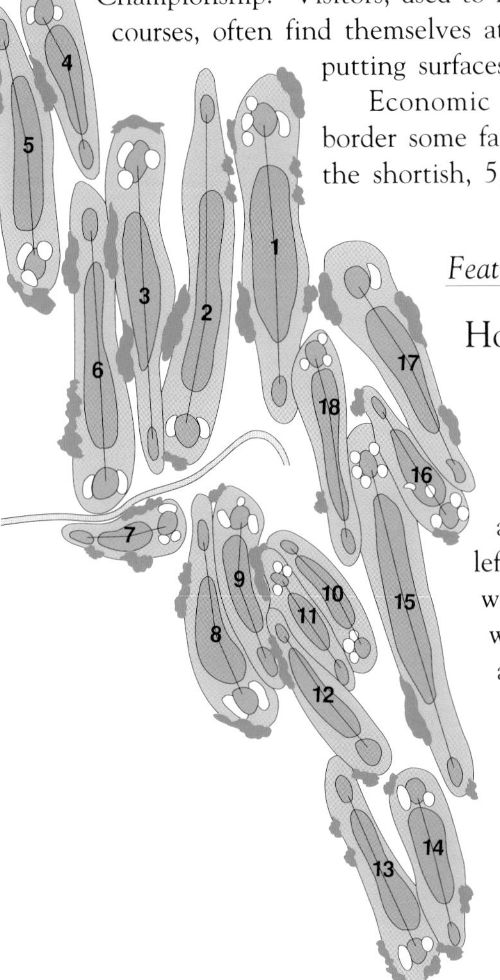


*Featured Holes:*

### Hole 1 - 423 Yards Par 4

From this elevated tee you get a beautiful view of Waikiki. A ridge runs from right to left across the fairway, but has a lesser slope on the left side. The ridge is known as "old man's hill." The clever player drives left of center, but don't overdo it as there is water down the left side. With the trade-winds behind, a 3-wood could fly the ridge and give you a 150–160-yard second shot onto a well-bunkered green. The water hazard is still on your left, but at this stage, not in view. There is plenty of slope on the green to arrest the shot, so balloon a short iron in.

*(above) Oahu is a hilly course with unforgiving out-of-bounds areas. Here the 1st tee.*

## Hole 5 - 270 Yards Par 4

This hole is a little meaner. It is uphill and up wind. A lot of trees on the right, dominated by a huge banyan tree, and a bunker that can be reached on a quieter day are there to greet you on the tee. On the left of the fairway is another giant tree, trying to subtly coax you to aim right. Don't; even though the lie is level and inviting, you can see neither the pin, the green, nor the bunker in front — so keep left. This now allows you to play a basic 9-iron to a comfortable green.

## Hole 8 - 331 Yards Par 4

You are now on the elevated tee of one of the hardest par fours in Hawaii. The right side of the fairway is somewhat restricted by water and the left side is guarded by two giant monkeypod trees. There is also a creek running across where a good drive would normally land. The solution: a strong 3-iron off the tee, aimed left of center. So, you think that was difficult? Totally disregarding the seven bunkers protecting the elevated green, and the fact that your approach, from 150 yards out, is narrowed by the influence of trees, hit an 8-iron onto this attractive green, which is surrounded by white and red ginger, bamboo, and a variety of other flora.

*(above) The 3rd green: a quick respite of width. Don't expect it to last long.*

## Hole 14 - 442 Yards Par 4

You are now standing on the highest point of the course and being welcomed by Hang-about, a semi-tame mongoose. Looking greenward, the fairway appears to have been contoured into a double dog-leg. On the right side of the fairway are two large trees. Use these as the target for your drive. The trades should then guide your ball gently to the middle. Having now enjoyed possibly the longest drive you have hit in a long time, all that is needed for your 130-yard second is a 9-iron to the well-defined green. Just be careful of the two hidden bunkers in front.

## Hole 15 - 574 Yards Par 5

Hole 15 is what one might describe as a spinnaker hole because of the elevated tee, with the fairway down wind, downhill. With plenty of height and power in your drive you could make the 574 yards in just two shots. Still, with 240 yards to go, thump a solid 3-wood to this green that stands up at the back. If you don't quite make it in two, no problem. It's still a one-putt birdie or a very comfortable five.

*The 13th green at Oahu Country Club. Ring the bell on the right when you've finished putting, so anybody in the swale below will know it's safe to hit.*

# OLOMANA
## GOLF LINKS

Olomana Golf Links is one of the few courses in the country where cattle come into play. Well, at least they'll be watching you play a couple of the holes on this rural, windward Oahu golf course.

Set near the far eastern tip of the island, between the towns of Kailua and Waimanalo, the Olomana course was designed by Bob Baldock, whose signature is also on the Hickam Malama Bay and Mililani courses. It is a popular course among residents of Oahu, catering to roughly 100,000 rounds of golf yearly.

With the dramatic Koolau mountains rising directly behind the course, the scenery can be distracting. But keep your wits about you and your mind on golf because even though the course is relatively flat, it can be challenging. This is particularly true when the wind picks up.

Also, if water makes you nervous, you'll be nervous: there is a water system which runs common to many of the holes on the course. On eight holes—primarily on the back nine—it requires carry, generally from the tee. There is also a short water carry on the 15th, although this water hazard is not connected to the others.

*(below) Olomana is a pretty course set against the Koolau mountains. Here the 18th green and approach.*

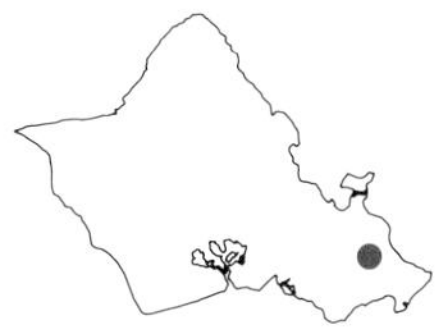

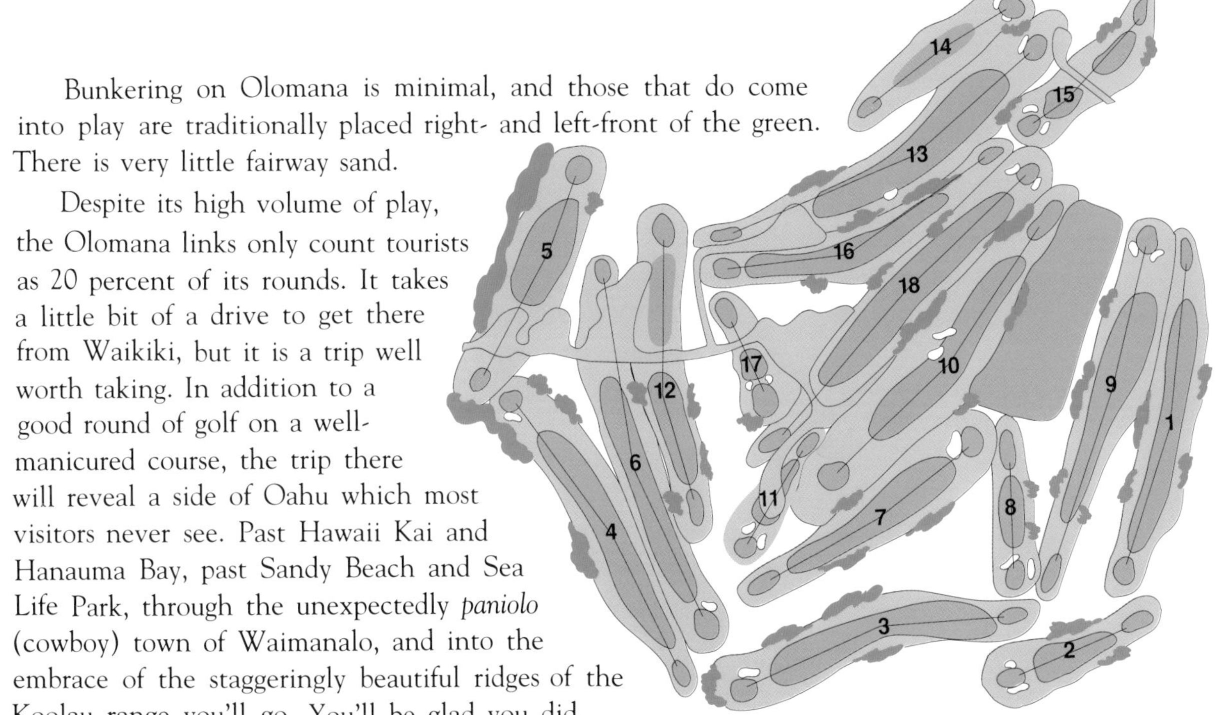


Bunkering on Olomana is minimal, and those that do come into play are traditionally placed right- and left-front of the green. There is very little fairway sand.

Despite its high volume of play, the Olomana links only count tourists as 20 percent of its rounds. It takes a little bit of a drive to get there from Waikiki, but it is a trip well worth taking. In addition to a good round of golf on a well-manicured course, the trip there will reveal a side of Oahu which most visitors never see. Past Hawaii Kai and Hanauma Bay, past Sandy Beach and Sea Life Park, through the unexpectedly *paniolo* (cowboy) town of Waimanalo, and into the embrace of the staggeringly beautiful ridges of the Koolau range you'll go. You'll be glad you did.

# PALI
## GOLF COURSE

On Oahu's windward side, in the shadow of the majestic Koolau mountain range, sits the 18-hole Pali Golf Course. It is situated with panoramic views of windward Oahu's most populous towns: during the course of a game, golfers will enjoy spectacular views of the cliffs of the Koolau range on one side, and the towns of Kailua and Kaneohe on the other.

Pali welcomed its first golfers in 1953. The 6,494-yard par 72 layout was designed by Willard Wilkinson and when it opened for play it was the third municipal course on Oahu. Now there are five with the newest, West Loch, having opened in 1990.

Although Pali is not a particularly difficult course, the layout makes use of the plentiful hills and valleys located throughout the more than 250 acres on which it is built. If anything, it is these undulations which challenge the skills of the golfer. Many balls, whether well-struck or not, will come to rest in a swale, and more likely than not you'll be shooting uphill much of the day.

*(below) The Koolau mountains form a dramatic backdrop for the Pali Municipal Golf Course. The 10th hole, pictured here, is not as hilly as most of the rest of the course.*

Unlike the newer resort courses found throughout the state, Pali has no man-made ponds or water features and very few sand traps. It does however, have a small stream which meanders through the course.

The challenge of the course is often increased due to adverse weather conditions: because of its location at the base of the Koolaus, Pali is subject to strong winds and frequent showers. Still, it is this same climate that helps to maintain the lush flora which beautifies the course.

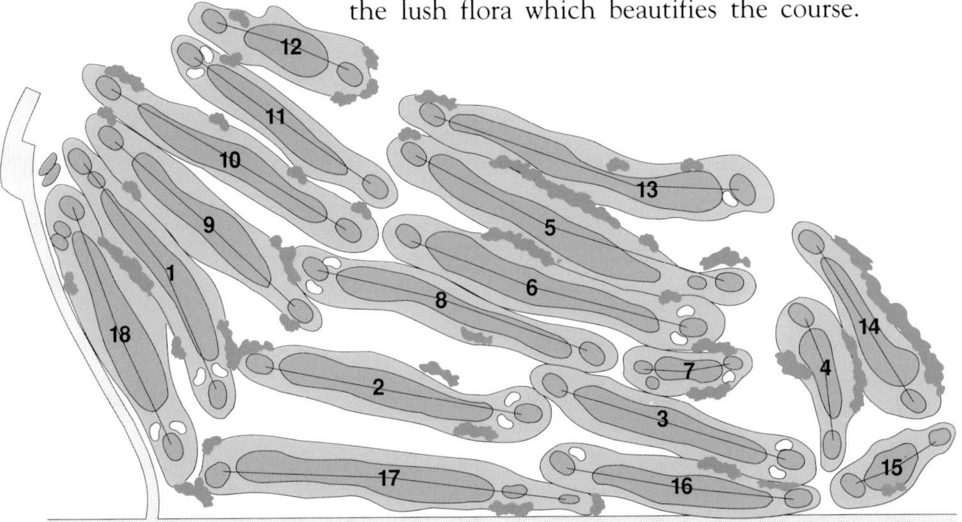

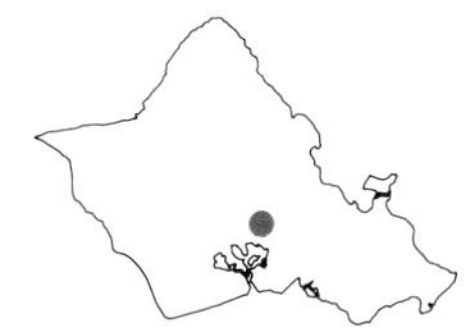

# PEARL
## COUNTRY CLUB

*(left) Pearl Country Club is one of the most popular courses on the island among local residents. Here, a view of the 9th green.*

The Pearl Harbor area is now ringed with seven golf courses, some military, some not. The Ford Island Golf Course, in fact, sits right in the middle of the harbor. And overlooking it all, from its seat in the Koolau foothills, is the Pearl Country Club, a non-military, semi-private course.

A beautiful 18-hole, 6,750-yard layout (from the championship tees), Pearl Country Club opened for play in 1967. Now, it is among the favorite courses of Oahu golfers, fielding some 80,000 rounds annually. Reservations can be made up to one month in advance, and should be if you're planning on playing a popular tee time.

Not until you reach the 503-yard par five 5th do you actually find a considerable challenge. Playing from an elevated tee, the hole dog-legs sharply left, with the first part of the dog-leg sloping severely downhill to the right. There is out-of-bounds on the uphill side, and a little stream comes into play on the right, after you've negotiated the turn in the dog-leg. The green, which you're more than glad to see after all this, is resting coyly in the shade at the end of the long haul, and does not present much more challenge to your putting out.

Hole 17 is a 518-yard par five which dog-legs left around some out-of-bounds apartment driveways. The safe way to play this hole is to the right. The problem is club selection. If you use your driver and play right, you face the possibility of slicing into the driving range. This is not a penalty at Pearl. You are asked only to drop closest to where you crossed the boundary. I say go for it left, aiming at the high point of the chain link fence which keeps you away from the apartments. A well-hit ball in that direction will give you a 75-yard advantage over the golfer who hit into the driving range.

From the highest points of the course, you are treated to spectacular views of Pearl Harbor, the Arizona Memorial, and the glittering Pacific Ocean beyond.

*The 11th green at Pearl Country Club on an exquisite golfing day, with Pearl City and Pearl Harbor in the background.*

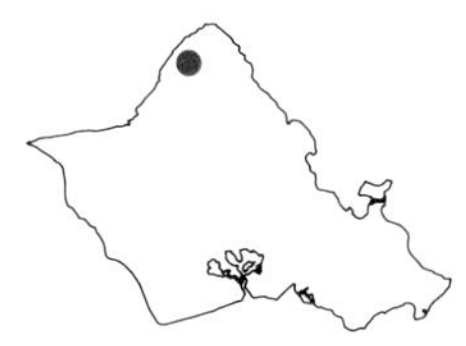

# TURTLE BAY
## COUNTRY CLUB

This resort course is on Oahu's farthest northern tip, and close to several of the most prestigious surfing beaches in the world: Sunset Beach, Waimea Bay, Haleiwa, and the Banzai Pipeline.

It takes about an hour to drive to Turtle Bay from Waikiki, through miles of pineapple and sugarcane fields. The resort is located on a dramatic point of land at the tip of an arching bay with white sandy beaches on either side.

The hotel was originally built by Del Webb, who wanted to operate it as a casino. This was not allowed by the state of Hawaii, and it subsequently became known as the Hyatt Kuilima. Currently, Hilton is the operator.

Being on the northern side of any Hawaiian island puts you on the windy side. This is true at Turtle Bay, although course professional Gary Brown says extensive planting of ironwood trees has helped ease the pain of a constant battle with the breeze.

The course was originally designed by George Fazio, but several others have also had a go at renovations, including Arnold Palmer, who has designed a new course to replace the existing course.

Insist on playing from the back tees before you part with your green fees. The course is very busy, and to push the numbers through the turnstile, the tees are often placed so far forward that none of the fairway hazards become a factor.

The current course is relatively flat, but measures a testing 7,036 yards. Within two years, however, the entire course layout will be changed.

*(left) The 11th green at Turtle Bay on Oahu's far north shore.*

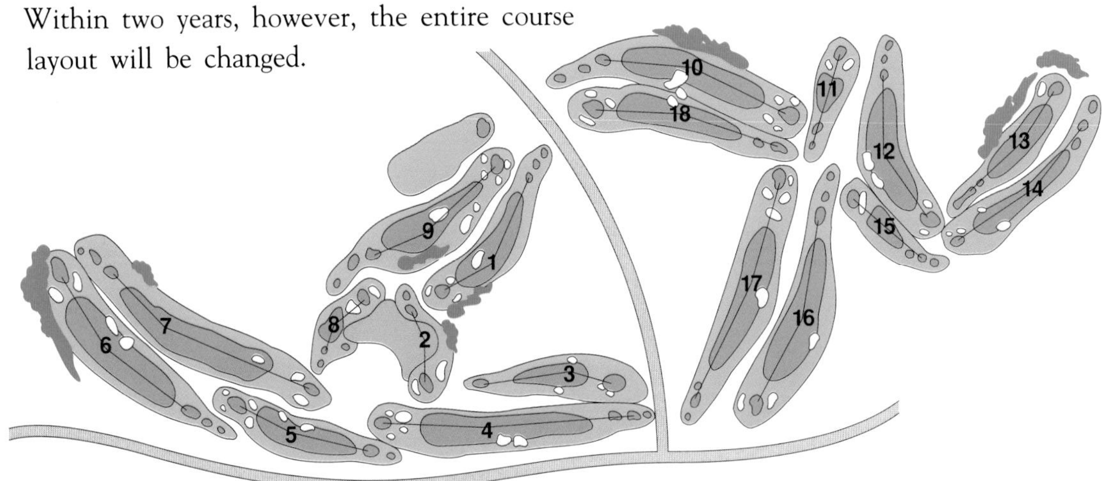

*Playing the 216-yard par three 2nd hole at Turtle Bay requires a little water carry. Concentrate.*

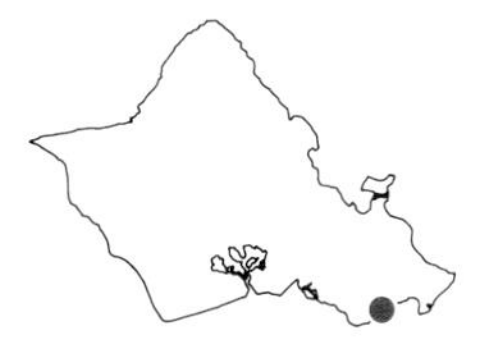

# WAIALAE COUNTRY CLUB

Any book on golf in Hawaii must include a review of the Waialae golf course –after all, it was near a bunker on the 10th hole where Private Prewitt (Montgomery Clift) was "shot" during the filming of *From Here to Eternity*.

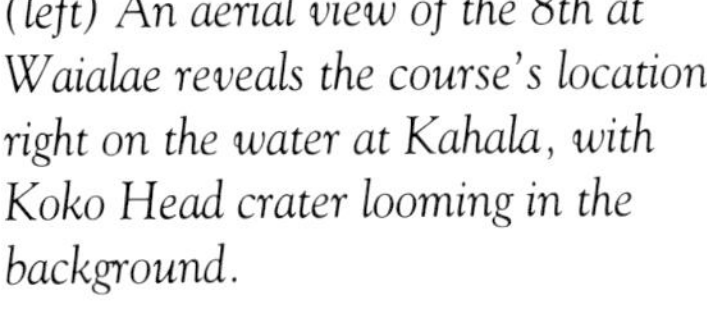

*(left) An aerial view of the 8th at Waialae reveals the course's location right on the water at Kahala, with Koko Head crater looming in the background.*

Most Americans, however, know Waialae because of the Hawaiian Open. Each February, the championship is bounced off satellite, and tens of thousands of golf fans in the northern hemisphere watch their television sets with frustration and envy, according to the depth of the snow in their driveways.

But while television makes Waialae one of the better-known courses in Hawaii, it is far from the best layout on the islands. It is a flat and relatively uninteresting course unless the tradewinds blow up a challenge.

But the flat fairways are well-groomed and the greens are slick and true. In fact, the fairways are so flat that during the years of World War II the Hawaiian Open was played at other courses because Waialae's fairways were strung with barbed wire to prevent landings by enemy aircraft.

The course was designed by Seth Raynor, a protege of C.B. Macdonald, the St. Andrews-trained architect who was a major influence in the growth of the game in America at the turn of last century.

Raynor drew up his plans in 1926, trying to include a smattering of Scottish-style moulding, which never really resembled the real thing because he died before he could see his vision take shape.

At 6,881 yards, the layout is a fairly short championship course in PGA terms. The secret of winning, or scoring well, is to conquer the par fives.

So if you are lucky enough to get a game (a tip is that if you are a Royal Hawaiian Hotel guest, a game can be arranged by the concierge), tackle the par fives as if you own them.

Another tip is to have a look at the sprinklerheads on the fairways. You will find yardages printed there with which you can gauge the clubs needed to reach the excellent putting surfaces.

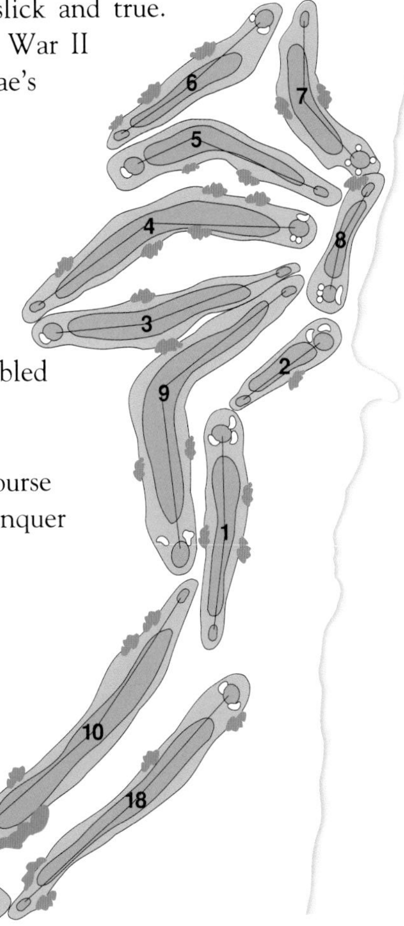

*(above) As can be seen from this photo of the 2nd green, Waialae is generally flat, and always well-groomed.*

*Featured Holes:*

## Hole 4 - 500 Yards Par 5 *"Akau"* (To the Right)

This extreme dog-leg right starts off into wind. A hidden trap on the dog-leg will prevent long hitters from cutting the corner. The green can be reached in two, but the second shot will require an accurate 3-wood to 3-iron shot into a cross wind to a large green sloping from back to front.

## Hole 5 - 407 Yards Par 4 *"Hema"* (To the Left)

Another severe dog-leg to the left. Again, a long trap guards the corner of the bend. The length of the second shot is dependent upon the placement of your drive and could vary from a 4- to an 8-iron. The large and slightly raised green, sloping decidedly from back to front, is guarded by hidden traps left and right.

## Hole 7 - 434 Yards Par 4 *"Welo"* (To Float in the Wind)

This dog-leg skirts the sea wall and is one of the prettiest holes on the course. A well-placed drive close to the kiawe tree on the left will leave a short iron or a wedge shot to the second largest green on the course.

*(above) The 7th green, looking back into the residential ridges of Honolulu.*

## Hole 9 - 539 Yards Par 5 "*Aloha*"

A possible birdie hole dog-legging severely left. The length of your second shot is dependent upon placement of your tee shot and the strength of the following wind. It can be a full 3-wood or as little as a 5-iron. Diamond Head looms majestically beyond the well-trapped green.

## Hole 15 - 458 Yards Par 4 "*Lalau*" (Go Astray, Get into Mischief)

A stiff par four against the wind with out-of-bounds on the right. A medium iron should be sufficient to reach the long, pear-shaped green which slopes from back to front, though the pin position can make a difference of as much as two clubs.

## Hole 17 - 419 Yards Par 4 "*Huluhulu*" (Hairy)

A tendency to play right on this dog-leg left is accentuated by a left-to-right cross wind. A trap awaits just such a tee shot. A wedge approach is all that is required to the trickiest green on the course, which is hard to hold if the pin is at the back.

*The site of the Hawaiian Open each year, Waialae Country Club is one of the most exclusive courses in Hawaii.*

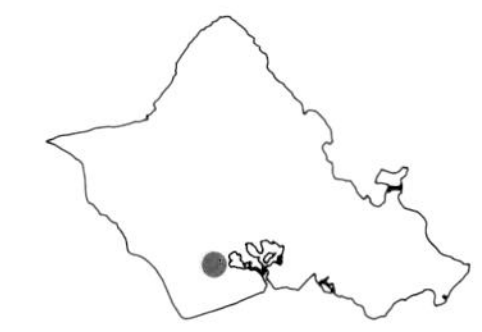

# WEST LOCH
## GOLF COURSE

*(left) The 495-yard, par five 2nd at West Loch fires around a lake. Stay right!*

On the southwest side of Pearl Harbor, approximately 30 minutes from Waikiki, sits the newest of the five municipal courses on the island of Oahu. The 18-hole, par 72 West Loch Golf Course opened for play in early 1990 and quickly gained popularity in a state where the demand for tee times greatly outstrips the supply.

Designed by Honolulu golf course architects Robin Nelson and Rodney Wright, it is the first municipal course to open since the nearby Ted Makalena course opened nearly 20 years prior. West Loch Golf Course, which sits in the midst of a residential housing area—West Loch Estates—utilizes the natural layout of the land to the fullest extent. The low elevation of the back nine—the course is bordered by the far western reaches of Pearl Harbor—requires extensive water drainage. Thus, drainage ditches and runoff ponds act as hazards on several holes.

It is an unusual layout in that the 1st hole plays right in front of the clubhouse, but then you have to drive under an expressway which divides the course to reach hole 2. You play holes 2 through 11 on this side of the highway, then switch back through the tunnel to play the final seven holes. Being a new course in 1990, the vegetation has yet to fully grow in. And the continuing development of new housing in the area will give the course a rough effect for a few years to come.

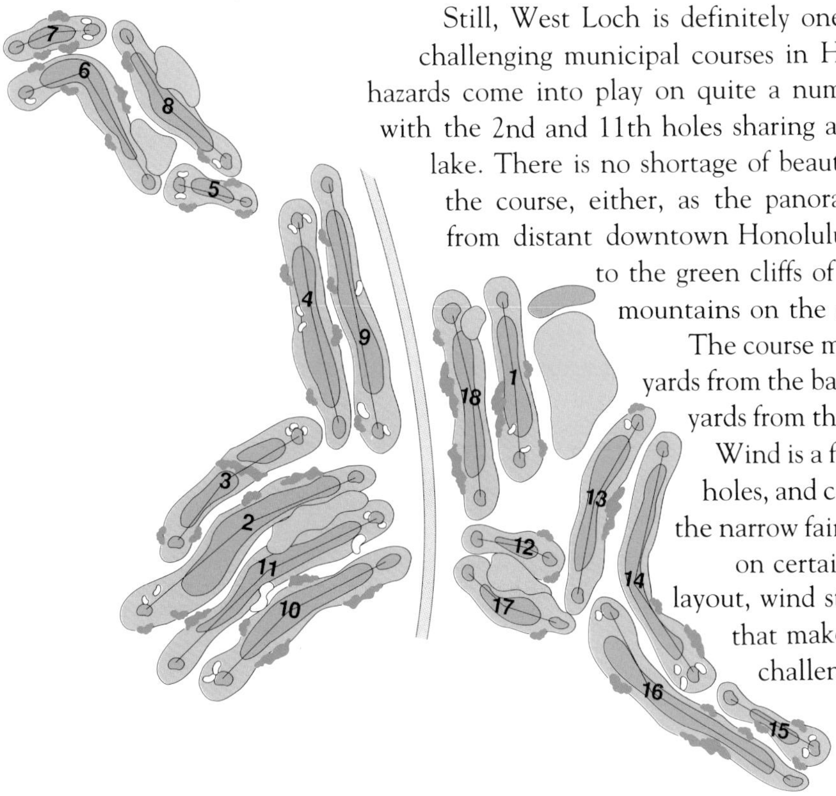

Still, West Loch is definitely one of the most challenging municipal courses in Hawaii. Water hazards come into play on quite a number of holes, with the 2nd and 11th holes sharing a large fairway lake. There is no shortage of beautiful vistas on the course, either, as the panorama stretches from distant downtown Honolulu on one side to the green cliffs of the Waianae mountains on the other.

The course measures 6,615 yards from the back tees, 6,070 yards from the middle tees. Wind is a factor on most holes, and combined with the narrow fairways featured on certain parts of the layout, wind strength is one that makes West Loch challenging.

ISLAND OF

# MOLOKAI

On a clear day you can see the island of Molokai, a mere 22 miles from Honolulu. And, while it is only nine miles from the hustle and bustle of Maui, Molokai remains relatively undiscovered by those seeking a Hawaiian holiday.

Molokai is the fifth largest of the Hawaiian Islands, about 38 miles long, 10 miles wide, with 88 miles of coastline.

The island's only town, Kaunakakai, looks like a set out of the wild west, yet it has a distinctive Hawaiian history. The most arable land on the island is owned by the 70,000-acre Molokai Ranch. The Ranch Safari — a tour available to Molokai visitors — showcases 400 wild animals, mostly imported from the savannahs of Africa.

# KALUAKOI
## GOLF COURSE

The Kaluakoi Golf Course, skillfully designed by Ted Robinson, is the best-kept golfing secret in Hawaii.

It is rarely crowded, and golfers often swim between shots along the five holes which prowl along Kepohui Beach, a gorgeous, long strip of white sand on the Pacific.

Other holes on the 6,618-yard, par 72 layout are surprisingly rolling, as they back into the gentle foothills, where one might encounter wild turkey and wild deer, which were a gift long ago from a Japanese emperor.

It is a course in a romantic setting and, in Robinson's view, is the "most spectacular and unusual course in the islands. Nature really designed the course, we just helped it along."

The adjoining resort is mellow. Your main impulse after the course has had a day or two to test your skills, is to go outside and fall asleep on the soft grass.

All in all, Kaluakoi is one of the most outstanding courses and restful resorts in the Hawaiian Islands. There are no elevators, no traffic lights or jams, and no city noise. Just peace, quiet, and tranquility.

Molokai's only other course is Ironwood, a fun, nine-hole, 2,790-yard, par 35 affair, run by the Del Monte Corporation in Kualapuu.

*(left) Kaluakoi's 3rd green, with long stretches of untouched white sand beach in the background. If your golf game is not working, maybe taking a long walk is a better idea.*

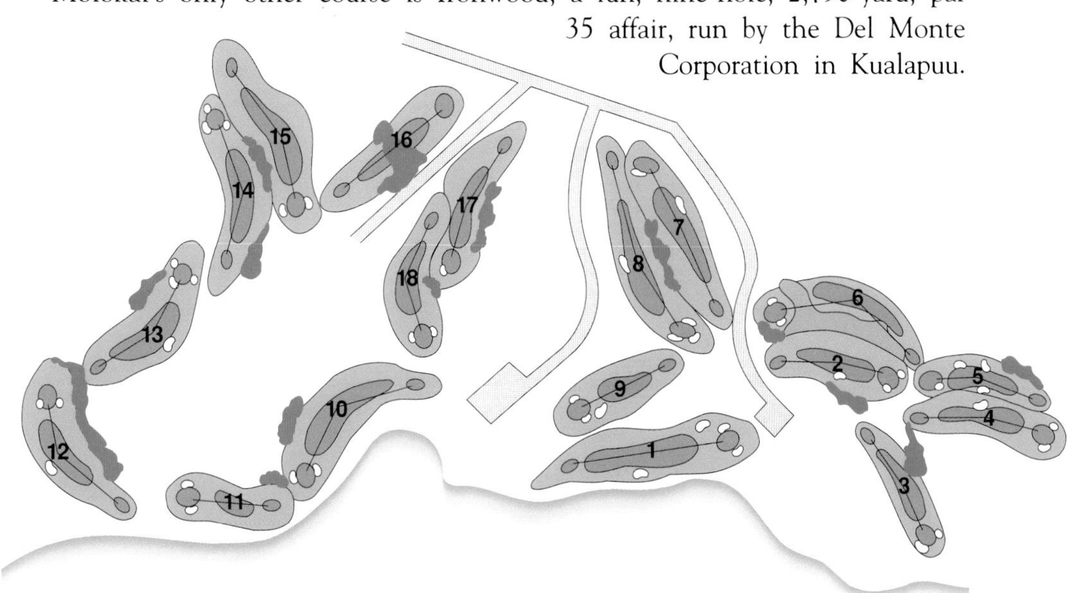

*(above) The approach and 4th green on the leisurely course at Kaluakoi.*

*Featured Holes:*

## Hole 1 - 505 Yards Par 5

The ocean and Kepohui Beach run alongside the right side of this fairway. It's a breathtaking view which can cause an immediate lapse of concentration even before your first tee shot.

But gather your thoughts and aim for a spot about 10 paces to the right of the bunker on the left. If you are feeling strong, you can carry your tee shot over the bunker on the right.

The opening hole offers a good birdie opportunity. It is 230 yards to the green from the front of the left bunker, and the day I played, I hit my second shot with a 16-degree metal club onto the green, but missed an eagle chance because I allowed for too much borrow with the putt. The lesson learned immediately on the first green was that the putts on Kaluakoi, for some odd reason, seem to run more truly than they do on other island greens.

Fan palms on both sides of the fairway indicate 150 yards to the green.

## Hole 4 - 408 Yards Par 4

Another great view. The spectacular white sand Papohaku Beach is on the right, so it is essential to keep your tee shot in play between bunkers left and right, which come into play. It is 180 yards to the green from the front of the bunker on the right. Shots hit left will be blocked by kiawe trees.

*(above) A dramatic ocean view is your treat on the 3rd tee.*

## Hole 10 - 396 Yards Par 4

Well, what have we here? Trouble on the right, the ocean on the left, and trouble behind the green. I used a 3-wood from the tee to prevent running out of fairway on the right. The tee shot is over a gorge, with the beach and rocks all along the left. There are two fan palms — the one on the right is 171 yards from the green; it is 150 yards from the palm on the left. The elevated green looks superb on the headland, with its backdrop coconut palms and blue sky. There are lovely ocean and beach views on three sides of the green. This is the windiest part of the course, which can affect your second shot, sweeping it towards the rocks and beach.

## Hole 11 - 136 Yards Par 3

You can hear the pounding of the ocean on the lava as you tee up. There is a rocky shore on the left-hand side, with bunkers front-left and right. Club selection is vital. The wind can whip your ball to the left and onto the beach behind the green. If you are not playing well you can retire to the beautiful swimming beach on this hole. Be careful of the downhill putt from the rear of the green.

ISLAND OF

# LANAI

The island of Lanai has long been known more for its pineapples than for its golf. In fact, pineapples cover the landscape from one end of this tiny island to the other. Lanai even derives its nickname — the Pineapple Island—from its prolific output of this sweet fruit.

But things are changing. Lanai will still grow pineapples, but resort development is also entering the economy. Two new hotels, the Lodge at Koele and the Manele Bay Hotel, have been built. And along with the hotels, two fabulous new golf courses are available to visitors.

The first, called the Experience at Koele, opened in January, 1991. It is an upcountry course, designed by Greg Norman and Ted Robinson. The second, at sea level, is called the Challenge at Manele, designed by Jack Nicklaus.

# LANAI COURSES

Lanai is most often referred to as the Pineapple Island, because it is home to more than 16,000 acres of pineapple and only 2,000 people. Privately owned by Castle & Cooke's Dole Pineapple company, the island is a rugged terrain with more than 100 miles of roads—although only 20 of those miles are paved. The economy of this tiny island has long relied on the plentiful harvests of sweet pineapple. Until very recently, Lanai was virtually untouched by tourism. The only hotel was a small, 10-room complex visited by rare adventurers seeking to discover the "untouched" Hawaii.

Today, that is changing. Two developments by Castle & Cooke's subsidiary, Oceanic Properties, entice visitors to experience Lanai and its new amenities: the Manele Bay Hotel, which rests on the western shore of the island, and the Lodge at Koele, nestled in the central highlands near Lanai City. Both offer spectacular golf courses.

The 102-room Lodge at Koele features a rare upcountry Hawaiian setting, an extensive collection of Pacific art, as well as Japanese and Hawaiian gardens of abundant island fruit. A challenging 18-hole championship course, known as the Experience at Koele, was built as part of the new luxury resort complex.

*(below) Brand new on Lanai, the Pineapple Island, is the Lodge at Koele, featuring an 18-hole Greg Norman-designed course. Here a view of the lodge.*

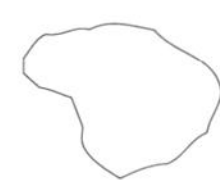

The Experience at Koele takes full advantage of the natural highland terrain. Mature Norfolk and Scotch pine trees beautify the course as well as add some unexpected challenges for the golfer. The Koele course offers breathtaking views of the Pacific Ocean on the front nine holes and the beautiful mountain valleys on the back nine.

The 162-acre course, which opened in January of 1991, was designed by Australia's "Great White Shark," Greg Norman, with golf architect Ted Robinson. Unlike other Hawaiian golf courses the Experience at Koele was first sown with Bent grass rather than Bermuda. The resort also includes a unique 18-hole putting course.

Down at the coastline, adjoining the Manele Bay Hotel, is another new course called the Challenge at Manele, designed by Jack Nicklaus. Unlike the Koele layout, this course's oceanfront setting subjects it to the same strong wind conditions as other Hawaiian courses which overlook the Pacific.

Until the 1990s, the nine-hole Cavendish Golf Course was the only golf course on Lanai. Built in 1947, Cavendish served as a recreational facility to the small community of plantation workers living in the area and remains popular with Lanai residents to this day.

Like all of the Hawaiian Islands, Lanai offers beautiful beaches for visitors who enjoy sailing, snorkeling, diving and sunbathing. The most beautiful is the isolated Hulopoe Beach on the southeastern coast.

ISLAND OF

# MAUI

The Valley Isle offers its guests a potpourri of earthly delights. The main visitor area on the west side of the island is the Kaanapali strip, an area blessed with gorgeous white sand beaches, gentle surf, and some of the most elegant hotels to be found anywhere.

Just down the road from Kaanapali is Lahaina, an old whaling town which has been transformed in recent years into a center for arts and fine dining. Until the late 1850s, when it was moved to Honolulu, Lahaina was the capital of the kingdom of Hawaii. It is one of those lovely little Hawaiian towns which still retains its Old World flavor.

On the south side of the island, the resort areas of Wailea and Makena offer luxury accommodations, first-rate golf, and long stretches of white sand beaches.

The island of Maui is dominated by the dormant volcano, Haleakala, which reaches more than 10,000 feet into the Hawaiian sky. One of the spectacular side trips popular among visitors to Maui is a sunrise pilgrimage to the crater's rim. After you've done it, you'll understand why Haleakala in Hawaiian means "House of the Sun."

*The old whaling village of Lahaina is one of the favorite stops during a vacation to Maui.*

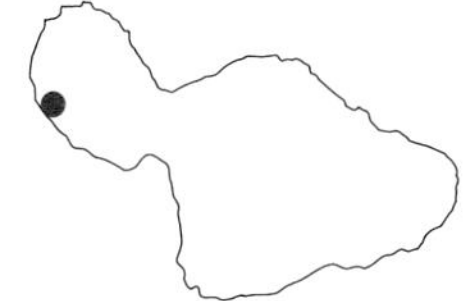

# KAANAPALI RESORT

Kaanapali was Hawaii's first planned resort area, the initial phase of hotel development commencing in the mid 1960s, with the building of the Sheraton Maui on famous Black Rock.

It is an area rich in history. The old Hawaiians populated the Kaanapali area, living in small villages along the coast. They were an isolated people, uninfluenced by the Western world. They fished, grew taro where the mountain streams fed into the ocean, and ardently followed the rituals and beliefs of their ancestors.

Today, the area is vastly different from that long-gone era. With roughly 6,000 rooms in more than a dozen top-flight hotel and condominium developments, two golf courses, and world-class shopping, the Kaanapali strip is Hawaii's second largest visitor destination, ranking after Waikiki.

The top hoteliers in the United States run properties in Kaanapali, including Hyatt, Sheraton, Westin, and Mariott. It is an area which is extremely popular with group and convention business, as well as among travelers who simply wish to flop on the beach for a few days in the warm Maui sun.

Obviously, with all this activity, the golf courses are busy, with some 90,000 rounds played annually.

Just down the road are the old Pioneer Sugar Mill to remind visitors of the agricultural roots of Maui, and the historic whaling town of Lahaina. The Sugar Cane Train, which used to haul sugar to port at Lahaina, now hauls tourists between Lahaina and Kaanapali.

*(left) A rainbow illuminates the Royal Kaanapali North course. Even though Kaanapali boasts two of the busiest courses in the state, both are well kept up and provide a good challenge.*

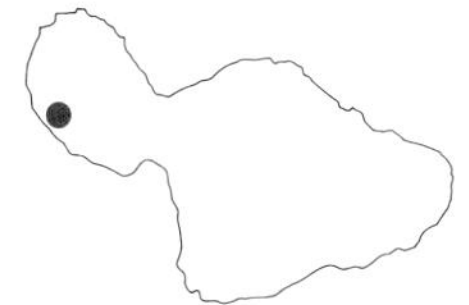

# THE NORTH COURSE

Royal Kaanapali's North course is a Robert Trent Jones, Sr. design which, when opened in 1962, set the style and standard for Hawaiian courses in the years to follow. His great layout at Mauna Kea on the Big Island came two years later.

The North course has all the earmarks of a Trent Jones layout: lots of big bunkers, long runway-type tees, and large, contoured greens.

It measures 7,179 yards, par 72. It features the largest and most highly contoured greens on Maui and is rated 75 from the back tees. Eight par fours are 412 yards or longer. Approach shots to the greens are critical on this layout, and it is important to leave yourself with uphill putts.

Heavy fairway and green bunkering also adds to the difficulty of the layout. The front nine overlooks the Pacific, while the back nine climbs into the misty mountains behind. Even at its highest point, though, the North course still has a panorama of the white sand beaches below.

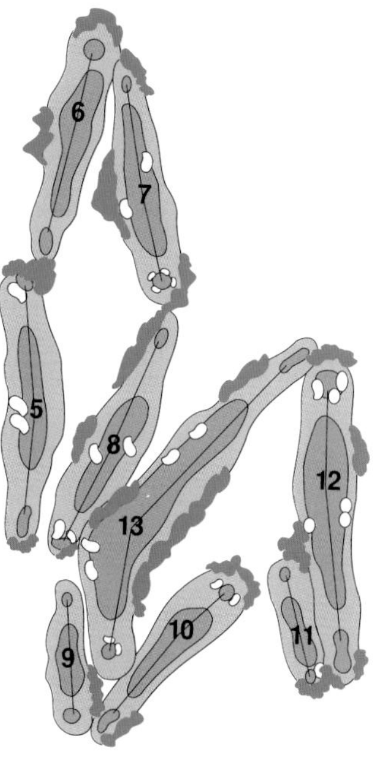


*(left) The par five 13th on the North course is a 645-yard monster with a beautiful view of the Kaanapali strip in the background.*

*Featured Holes:*

## Hole 3 - 427 Yards Par 4

With the breeze coming from your right, aim your tee shot down that side, following the row of trees. The bunker on your left is not reachable. For the 170 yards still remaining, hit a 5-iron with the breeze. Don't believe what you see—the green slopes from left to right. Totally ignore that as the grain, growing in the opposite direction, more than compensates.

*(above) Excellent golfing weather is a standard feature on this side of Maui. Here, the 1st tee, a 541-yard par five.*

## Hole 1 - 541 Yards Par 5

There is a water hazard on your right for almost the entire length of this hole. With the prevailing trades coming from the right, it is important that you drive right of center. This will position you on the bend of the dog-leg right. Do not be tempted to reach this hole in two, as the water hazard now cunningly sneaks unseen into the fairway just short of the green, making your second shot more than 200 yards of carry. Do what the sensible players do— lag up with a 5-iron. This should then leave you a firm punch shot into the breeze and against the grain to a green that runs on the oblique. Your club choice for this 50-yard shot will now only depend on the strength of the wind.

## Hole 13 - 645 Yards Par 5

Gather all your strength for this drive and aim it at the two bunkers on the right. The fact that the tee is elevated helps you snatch up a few bonus yards. Try to put some left-hand influence on your tee shot. With your 3-wood, your plan of attack is to miss the pine tree which guards the out-of-bounds on your left. You should then be in a grassy hollow which was not evident before, but it does not present any real problem. Just throw a wedge up onto this spacious green and putt.

*(above) The 15th at Kaanapali North dog-legs right, wind from the right. Easy: use your natural slice!*

## Hole 16 - 466 Yards Par 4

Check the sugarcane train timetable before you tee off here. Otherwise you could have a whistle blast in the middle of your backswing. This hole has the slightest of kinks on the left-hand side of an otherwise straight fairway. The kink is provided by a bunker and some palm trees, with the fairway sloping away from them. There is out-of-bounds on the left and water and out-of-bounds on the right. Direct your 3-wood at the banyan tree on the right. All that should then be required is a firm 9-iron onto this well-trapped green.

## Hole 18 - 438 Yards Par 4

Regarded as one of the most difficult finishing holes in Hawaii, the 18th demands respect, not by its distance, but its character. Water runs in front of the tee, along the right, then impinges just before the green, where it continues, bordering the right side of the green. It is very important that your drive finishes left of center, just missing the left-hand bunkers. From some 175 yards out, you are now confronted with a thinking shot. Think with a 5-iron. This green runs in length from left to right and is well-guarded. You need to aim left. If you are short, you are in the throat. Anything longer can only find its way to the center. Don't spoil a good card.

*The 466-yard par four 16th on Kaanapali North.*

# THE SOUTH
## COURSE

This course opened in 1970 as an "executive" course for high-handicap golfers. But in 1977, Jack Snyder was commissioned to transform it into a regulation championship layout.

Snyder expanded some holes, changed the course layout, and now, at 6,758 yards from the back tees, it requires accuracy on hilly fairways which are whipped regularly by tradewinds.

It is more picturesque than the North course because the holes are at higher elevations. In winter months, the channel waters between the islands of Maui, Molokai, and Lanai become a playground for the great humpback whale. And you can see it all from the fairways and greens.

*(below) With the island of Molokai rising in the distance, golfers face a wide-open 420-yard par four on the 9th at Kaanapali South.*

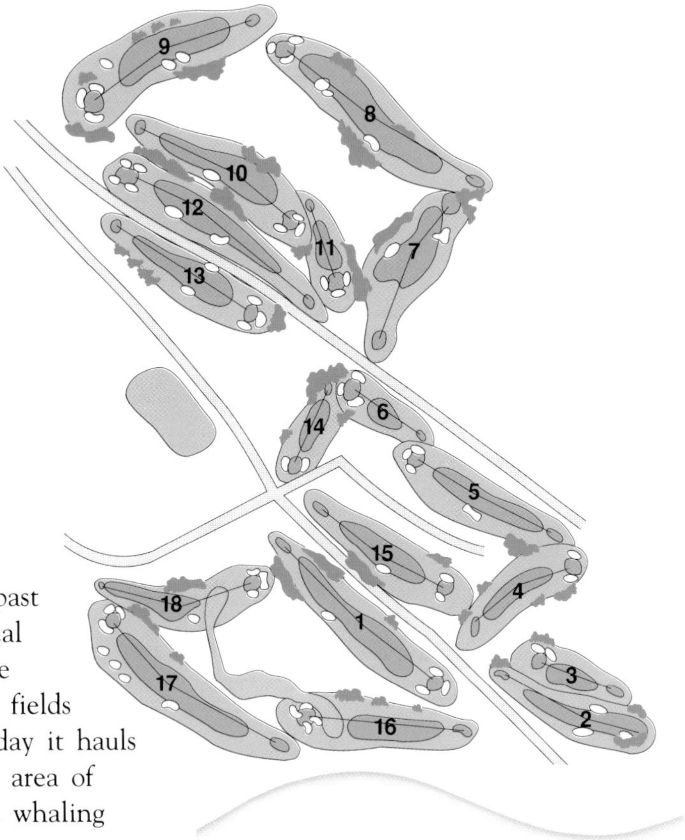

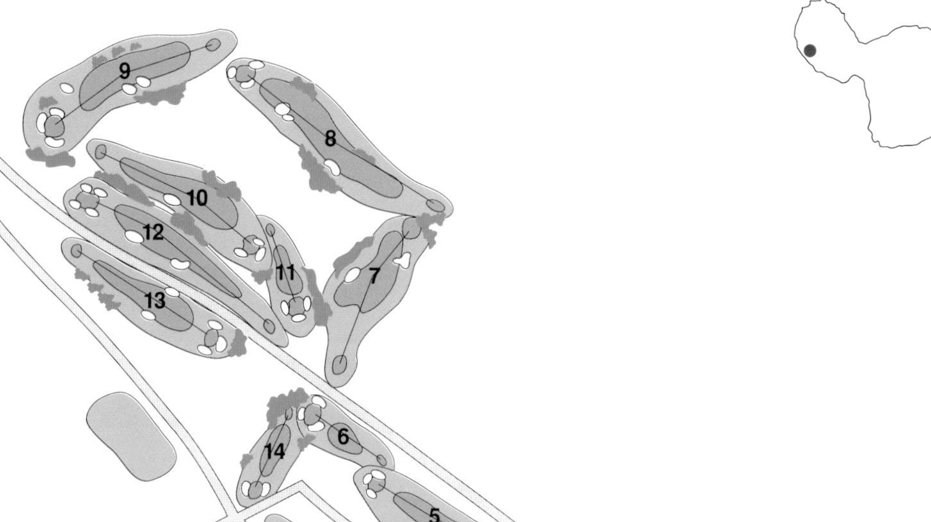


A steam locomotive, which occasionally chugs past the 4th, can be a whimsical distraction. This train once hauled sugarcane from the fields to the shipping docks. Today it hauls visitors between the resort area of Kaanapali and the historic whaling town of Lahaina.

*(above) Don't veer too far right! A 200-yard par three, the 11th at Kaanapali South wraps this ball-loving lake.*

*Featured Holes:*

## Hole 1 - 490 Yards Par 5

This is a good opening hole, not too difficult and it can be reached in two. However, the percentage way of playing it and ensuring a good start is to use a 3-wood off the tee and play it straight down the middle. To help you in this attempt, remember there is out-of-bounds all the way, both right and left. For your second shot, play a firm 2-iron to the neck of the green, which broadens out the further you go. At the very worst you are on the front edge: a good start.

## Hole 4 - 320 Yards Par 4

Everything on this short uphill par four goes from left to right. Tee up on the right side of the mound and aim for the two sprinkler boxes on your left. All those influences should contribute to centering your drive. If you take this advice, the out-of-bounds on either side of the fairway will not come into consideration. From down in this slight hollow, thump a short 9-iron up onto this rather spacious green, straight for its middle.

## Hole 9 - 420 Yards Par 4

You are now at the highest point of this course. It is all downhill and very picturesque. The blue Pacific is a backdrop, with the islands of Molokai, Lanai,

*(above) The Kaanapali strip borders the 16th hole, a 410-yard par four.*

and Kahoolawe in the distance. Nevertheless, you still have to concentrate on your drive. With out-of-bounds both right and left and driveable bunkers on the left, the ideal position for your second shot is just right of center. With 150 yards to go to the middle of the green, you have to contend with the fact that the flag is not only below you, but it is down breeze and the grain runs with the ball. The green is bunkered right, left and rear, and there is out-of-bounds in those areas as well. The green is built up on a mound and the ground runs away on all sides except the front. The only shot you have is to throw the ball up high onto the cut surface. Around the back of the green a mound has been built up just like a turned-up collar.

## Hole 18 - 350 Yards Par 4

An interesting finishing hole. The inevitable out-of-bounds both right and left dogs this hole all the way. On the outside of the left bend awaits a fairway bunker, and then a water hazard, both of which are driveable. Do not take a short-cut on this one. Take your 3-iron and bend it from the right side. Lag it up short of the water. You now have 150 yards of 7-iron aggression remaining. The reason for this attacking shot is that you cannot see the water hazard between you and the green. There is a bunker to the left, bunkers to the right, bunkers to the rear; but there is plenty of room on the green.

Always remember in this game: *Kulia i ka nu'u, i ka puepae kapu a liloa* – Strive to do your best.

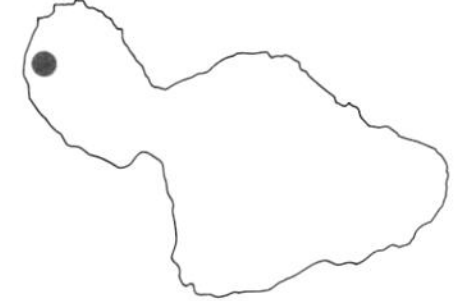

# KAPALUA RESORT

Kapalua Resort, six miles above Kaanapali, is perched on the northwestern tip of Maui. This exclusive resort community is comprised of three exquisite golf courses, a hotel, and a number of privately owned homes and condominiums.

The first two golf courses built at Kapalua have Arnold Palmer's signature attached to them: the Bay course, which opened for play in 1975, and the Village course, opened in 1980. A new layout—the Plantation course—designed by Ben Crenshaw and Bill Coore, opened in mid-1991, making Kapalua the only resort in Hawaii with three championship 18-hole courses.

The Plantation course is unique because of its size—it is situated on a massive 240 acres of sweeping hillsides and deep ravines. As on the other two Kapalua courses, golfers must split their time between being amazed spectators in a dramatically beautiful environment, and concentrating on their golf game.

Each year, Kapalua resort hosts a variety of events, some related to golf, some not. The Kapalua International (formerly Isuzu sponsored) occurs each November, and is part of the PGA tour. Then, one of the more popular events is the Kapalua Wine Symposium which occurs each July, bringing together many of the best winemakers from California with many of the top someliers in the country.

In Hawaiian, Kapalua means "arms embracing the sea." It is a name which befits this elegant resort both physically—as it sits on lava arms stretched out to the sea—and symbolically, as Kapalua takes great care and pride in maintaining a respectful relationship with the Hawaiian landscape and culture.

*(left) Kapalua resort, six miles northwest of Kaanapali, now features three championship 18-hole golf courses, a great hotel, and many homes and condominiums.*

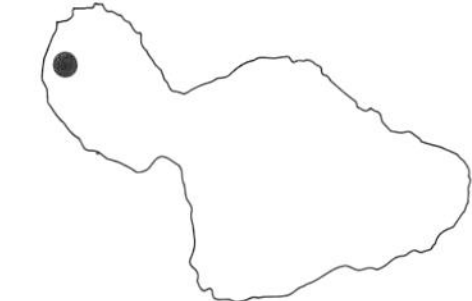

# THE BAY
## COURSE

The Bay course is a lovely layout surrounded by groves of coconut palms, ironwoods and Cook pines, a sandy coastline which can be seen from almost every tee and green, and thousands of acres of pineapple. It was designed by Arnold Palmer with Francis Duane. And, although it has been home to the Kapalua International golf championship, the course can be negotiated with pleasure by high handicappers.

*(left) The 12th tee on the Bay course requires a short carry to achieve the par of three.*

Completed in 1975, it measures 6,761 yards with a par of 72. The fairways, despite being long, are generous, and there is hardly a bad lie to be found. Still, there's just enough rough to keep the straying golfer honest, and the greens do their best to confound you.

What can make the course unpredictable is the weather; it's as fickle and temperamental as a spoiled brat. One minute blue skies and warm sun, the next a brief shower with a tricky ocean breeze.

There are many interesting holes, with the 5th probably the most photographed on the course – a par three with a rocky inlet and pounding surf. Try hitting your shot from the championship tee over the foaming surf to a well-bunkered green 205 yards away. But use one less club than normal, because the wind is usually behind.

Golfers who think their way around the layout should have little trouble playing to their handicap and therefore will have a good day on the Bay course.

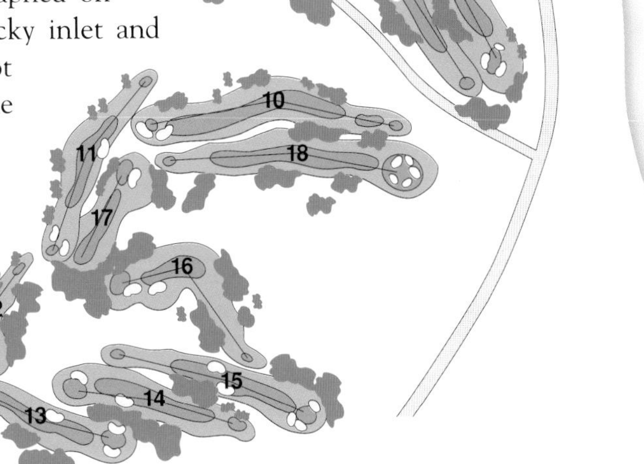

*(above) It's hard to imagine a more inviting scene than the 16th green of the Bay course. But watch out for pin placement: it's liable to be in the middle of a severe undulation.*

*Featured Holes:*

## Hole 5 - 205 Yards Par 3

Just think of one thing, *Oi ho'i he hana ha'awe o kaumapa* — It's no trouble at all. The fact that the Pacific Ocean comes between you and the green really should not alarm you. Take out your 3-iron, hit it with plenty of height at the little bit of cart path you can see on the left, and the prevailing conditions will bring it back onto the green. Don't worry if the ball seems to be dying short. The fact that the drying wind condition makes the ground a little hard will keep the ball bouncing.

## Hole 10 - 527 Yards Par 5

From this elevated tee, use the right side fairway bunker as a guide and keep it on your right by going straight down the center. As the ball loses velocity, the breeze will nurse your shot into the bend. Now, repeat that shot with your 3-wood aimed at the left-hand bunker, just short of the green. A wedge onto this generously bunkered green is not the problem, but where you place the shot is important. You must finish on the same level as the pin. The left half of the green is one level. Now divide the right half into two. The front section is the next level up and the remainder is the highest level. So the best advice is to be adjacent to the pin.

*(above) The 18th green is protected by bunkers right, left, and rear. If you're feeling conservative, lag up short and use your wedge to achieve this green.*

## Hole 15 - 470 Yards Par 4

This hole has plenty of character. The scenery is breathtaking. Jungle lines the right and there are trees on the left, one of which stands in the middle of a concealed bunker. There is another concealed bunker on the right. When you have finished admiring the view, hit your driver straight at the peak of Molokai. That is, if it's a clear day. If not, try 20 yards to the right of the flowering tree on your left. It is important that you do this, as you cannot see the fairway. Having middled your drive, play your 9-iron in from the left-hand side.

## Hole 18 - 552 Yards Par 5

Pause for a moment and absorb the vista. Progressively—you have fairway, green, clubhouse, Pacific Ocean, and Molokai. By utilizing the tail wind and hitting height into your driver, sail it down the right side and you will be within a 5-wood of reaching this green in two. If you are going for it, play the 5-wood exactly the same way as the driver. There is a narrow throughway onto this six-bunkered green. If you are a little conservative and want to keep your good score intact, play a 4- or even 5-iron and lag up safely.

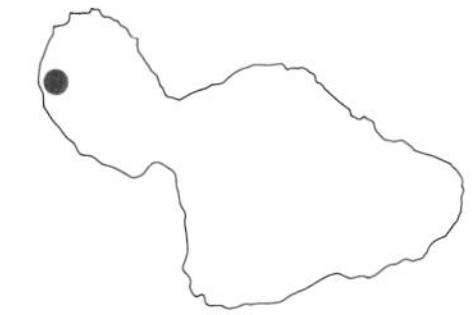

# THE VILLAGE
## COURSE

Arnold Palmer teamed with Ed Seay to build the Village course, which takes the golfer 800 feet into the West Maui mountains to mingle with pineapple fields and Cook pines.

The 5th and 6th holes of the 6,632-yard, par 71 layout, which opened in 1980, could easily be the most scenic in Hawaii. They are built along a narrow ridge with spectacular views of the Pacific, specifically Honokahu Bay, Makalapuna Point, Oneloa Bay, and a spray of green pineapple fields.

Club selection plays a big part of the game on this course, since holes play uphill, downhill and the stiff wind, depending on direction, can make hitting unpredictable. In fact, I enjoy this course more than the Bay. You never seem to play the same shot twice on any hole.

And watch the break on the greens. The normal break is toward the channel between the islands of Molokai and Lanai.

*(left) The 5th tee on the Village course demands your attention. A dog-leg left with water nearby, you might want to consider using your 2-iron to get around the bend.*

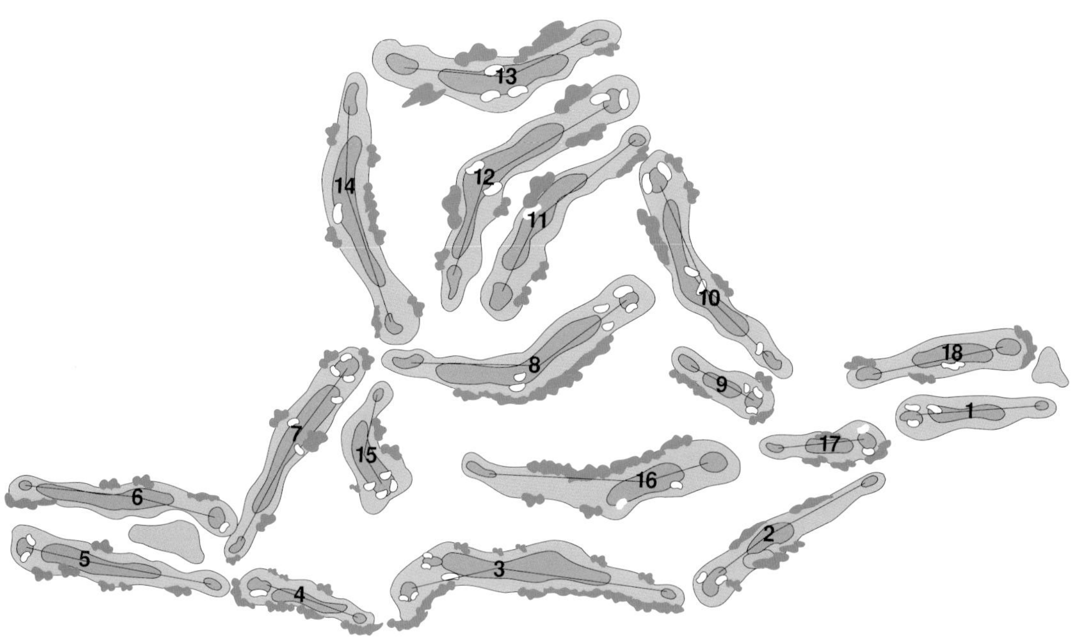

*(above) A downhill par four, the Village 7th gives a good idea of the elevation of this course.*

*Featured Holes:*

## Hole 3 - 514 Yards Par 5

This hole is the hardest on the Village course. It is rather narrow and tends to look that way due to the dense vegetation along both sides. You will need a good, well-directed, low, wind-cheating drive to get a respectable distance up the hill. The probabilities of a birdie here increase if you lay up with a 3-iron, rather than go for the green with a 3-wood and contend with the six bunkers. Having played your 3-iron to the right of the green, you should have an easy chip on, against the grain.

## Hole 6 - 367 Yards Par 4

The scenery here can get under your guard. Be alert. From up on the tee, play your driver down a corridor of stately pines which shelter your shot for the first 180 yards. Then the breeze whisks in from the right, so be down that side. Don't go wandering off to the right, or you will get your feet wet. In this exposed area, your 9-iron needs to be punched low and certainly not too gently to hold onto this fair-sized green.

*(above) This 367-yard par four runs down a corridor of stately pines. Don't fall short as you approach the green: you'll get your feet wet.*

## Hole 11 - 393 Yards Par 4

There is no fancy work required on this hole. It is uphill all the way and the fairway curves to the left, going in the same direction as the wind. Aim your driver to the right-hand fairway bunker and it will drift back. Do the same on your next shot with no less than a 4-iron and come in to the green from the right. Remember, you are still climbing.

## Hole 14 - 496 Yards Par 5

Put everything into low gear. Every yard gained is through endeavour and determination. Just grit your teeth and unleash your driver just left of the bunker that is visible. Even with all that effort, you are still 225 yards short of the green. But the ultimate destination is yet to reveal itself, so until it does, blast away with a 3-wood aimed at the right-hand edge of the row of Cook pines that provide a collar for the unseen green. Then, at long last you have something to play to. All that is needed is a flipped wedge, or if you feel more comfortable, a down-the-shaft 9-iron to earn yourself an easy five.

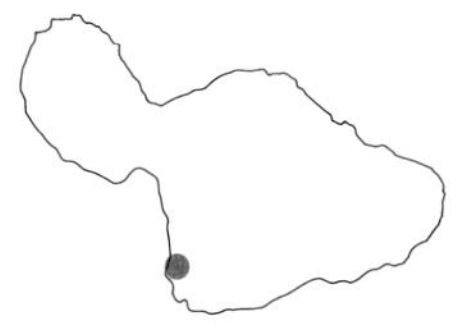

# MAKENA RESORT
## GOLF COURSE

Makena, on Maui's southwestern coast, some 40 miles south of the Kaanapali area, offers an excellent test of the game on a 6,739-yard, par 72, Robert Trent Jones, Jr.–designed layout.

You will need every club in the bag— and wish you had a few more— to negotiate the narrow, rolling fairways and the huge, fast, undulating greens.

There are four water hazards, 64 bunkers, and a couple of distractingly gorgeous ocean holes with views of Haleakala Crater. It is a magnificently groomed layout which covers 203 acres of land.

Trent Jones, Jr. did a good job with Makena. A round of golf on this layout, completed in 1981, is a stimulating experience, and you can plan a holiday there knowing it rarely rains.

It is an interesting area. Hawaii's King Kalakaua and Queen Kapiolani arrived at Makena aboard the S.S. *Kilauea* to visit Captain James Makee, the governor of Kapena, three days after the king's election to the throne in 1874.

They were greeted at Makena Landing by 150 horsemen carrying torches, standard bearers, singers, dancers, and attendants carrying *kahili* (feathered standards).

It became known as Makena, "the beach of mourning," after the fire goddess Pele, in her fury, sent lava from Haleakala to the sea.

The magnificent Makena resort is owned by Japan's Seibu Corporation, headed by Yoshiaki Tsutsumi, who, according to *Forbes* magazine, is the "world's richest man."

*(left) From the lava rough, a view of the approach and green of the 5th at Makena.*

*(above) The 10th at Makena is a 502-yard par five highlighted by a couple of small lakes, and a great view of the Pacific. Try to pay attention to your game.*

*Featured Holes:*

## Hole 4 - 178 Yards Par 3

This is a lovely hole! Downhill, tons of timber on both sides and at the back, and a kidney-shaped green with bunkers front-left and right-rear. The beauty of the hole comes from the water clinging to the front and along the right edge of the very long green. If the pin is at the back, a 5- or 6-iron is needed from the tee.

## Hole 6 - 212 Yards Par 3

Don't let the beautiful view of Molokai take you away from your responsibility: smacking a strong mid-iron to this green, 60 feet lower than the tee. The green is bunkered left and right, so you cannot run the ball on. It is all carry to a slightly down wind and down-grain green.

## Hole 10 - 502 Yards Par 5

Big hitters will make this green in two. The fairway bends gently to the right, cuddling a large water hazard. On the outside of the bend, on your left, there is plenty of dense vegetation, and also a bunker, which under normal conditions

*(above) A typical Hawaiian golfing day: blue skies, well-groomed layouts, lush vegetation. Here, Makena's 18th. Want to go around again?*

would be out of range. The ideal tee shot here is to split the fairway. From there, lag up alongside the second water hazard which occupies the left side of the fairway, using your 4-iron. You should then be only 65 yards out, making it a simple exercise to hit the next shot onto the green, missing the front bunker.

## Hole 15 - 183 Yards Par 3

From the elevated tee here, you can plainly make out the free-form bunker nestling into the front right edge of the green. The water hazard just through the back of the green is the Pacific Ocean. Admire the view, then eyes down and concentrate on whether you are going to come in with the trades from the right, or from the left against the breeze, using the full length of the green. Use the club of your choice from the mid-range.

## Hole 16 - 383 Yards Par 4

If you don't finish right of center with your drive here, you could either be in the rough to the right or very wet to the left: the beautiful Pacific Ocean provides the left edge of this fairway. About 90 yards from the green, play a pitch-and-run shot because the green, the wind, and the grain all run from right to left. So a negative shot is the best way to handle this difficult set-up.

*The Makena side of Maui tends to get less wind.*
*Notice the near-perfect reflection of the trees in the water next to the 13th green. Don't shoot left here – you'll spoil the serenity.*

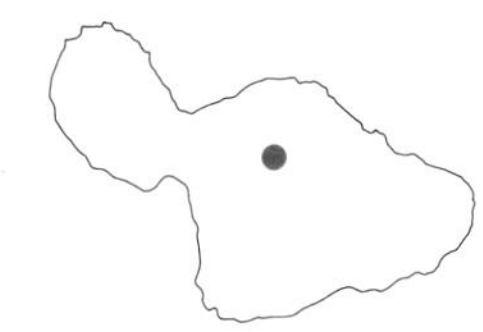

# PUKALANI
## COUNTRY CLUB

This layout is set in the rolling hillsides of upcountry Maui, overlooking the Pacific and the rest of the Valley Island from the 1,110-foot level of Haleakala.

The course, designed by Bob Baldock, measures 6,945 yards to a par of 72 and covers nearly 160 acres.

Pukalani is unique in that it has 19 greens. At the 3rd hole, golfers may choose from a tough shot across a gully and into the wind to one green, or choose an alternate, well-bunkered green several hundred feet below.

Water comes into play on two holes on the hilly layout which sports lush kikuyu grass fairways. At this altitude, it can get cool—so a sweater may be appropriate for early morning or late afternoon play.

The first nine holes of Pukalani opened for play in 1980, with the second nine coming on line four years later. The winds are a factor on this course, and you'll encounter quite a few hills and undulations. The trees at this elevation don't remind you much of Maui—instead of swaying palms, you'll find cypress and Norfolk pines.

The course offers a variety of interesting challenges. In addition to the unusual "two green" hole —the 3rd—you'll encounter a 500-yard par 4 at the 13th, and on the 4th. The 4th is made difficult by the fact that it's uphill all the way, and dog-legs to the left. There is out-of-bounds on both sides, and you're usually shooting against the wind.

Pukalani is a good round of golf, away from the crowd. It'll give the visitor an opportunity to see Maui from a vantage point most likely missed otherwise.

*(left) In the upcountry of Maui the Pukalani course can get a bit chilly. Bring a sweater. Here the 1st tee shoots downhill 454 yards to the green.*

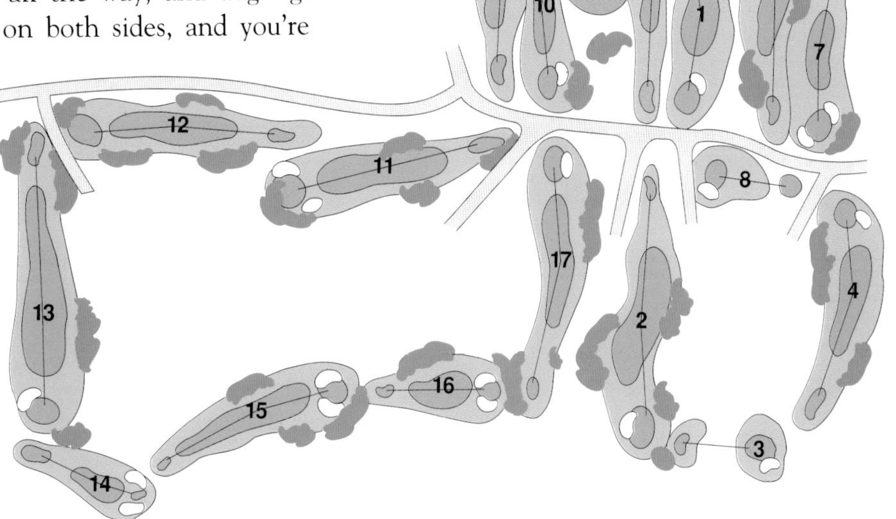

# SILVERSWORD
## GOLF CLUB

There are two things you can rely on with regards to golfing in Hawaii. The first is the incomparable beauty of the courses. And the second is that a new layout will be popping up somewhere very shortly.

Silversword Golf Club popped up in 1987, the second public course on Maui. It is located near Kihei, just down the road from the resort area of Wailea, on the leeward side of the island. The course is set somewhat back into the Haleakala foothills, and is subject to both the tradewinds coming from the Pacific and the afternoon winds which sweep from the mountain.

It is a par 71 course which measures 6,400 yards from the regular tees. Most of the front nine is laid out cross wind, with the majority of the back nine playing either with or into the teeth of the wind. Accuracy is more important than distance, and knowing how to adjust for wind conditions—if that is ever possible—is critical on Silversword.

*(below) Silversword is one of the newest additions to Maui's golf choices. Here on the 9th you get a pretty wide fairway, but with plenty of undulation.*

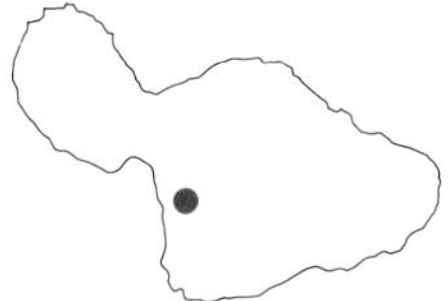

Fairway bunkering is minimal, although the greens are well-protected, often with three traps. Water comes into play on some holes, too, with holes 1 and 9 sharing a large lake which requires carry on both. Hole 13 has a lake just to the right of the green, and hole 15 is belted by two lakes at its waist.

The course is named Silversword after the Hawaiian fern of the same name which grows only in the higher elevations of Haleakala. Because of its setting above the town of Kihei, the course has great ocean views from almost every hole. If you are playing during the winter months, and if you have keen eyes, you're likely to be witness to one of the many pods of humpback whales which pass offshore.

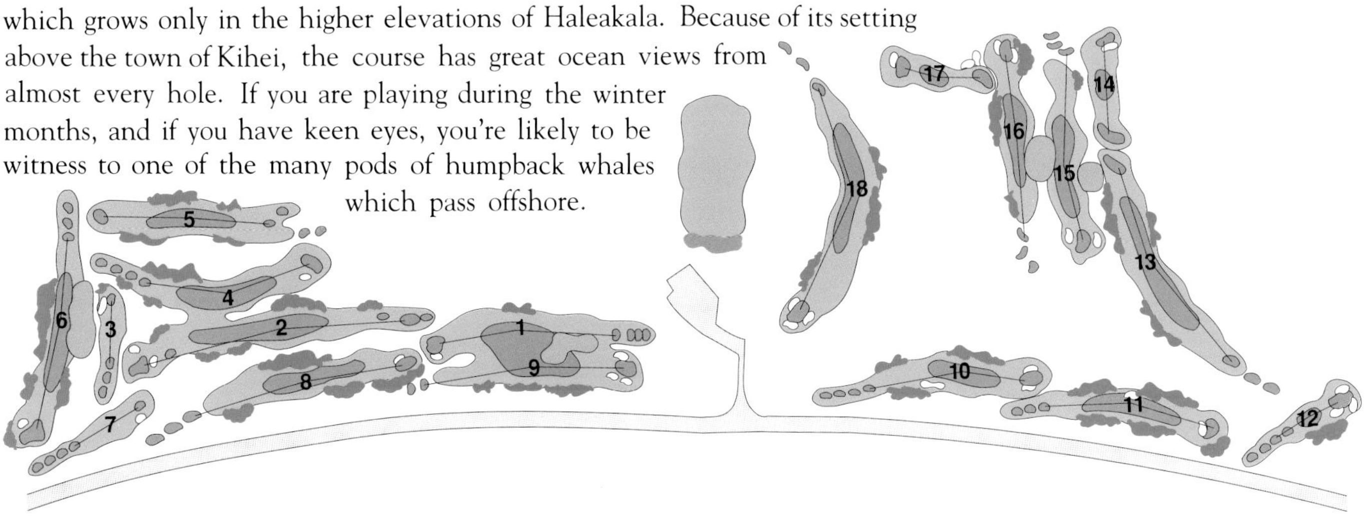

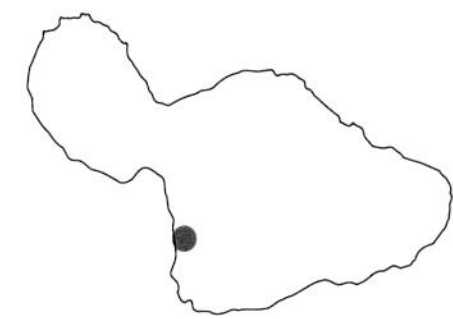

# WAILEA RESORT

Wailea offers two courses designed by Jack Snyder, the Orange and the Blue, both of which sprawl along gently rolling terrain, 40 miles south of the Kaanapali area on the sunny leeward Kihei coast.

In Hawaiian, Wailea means "Waters of Lea," after the goddess of canoe building. The traditional Hawaiians built canoes from the wood of the wiliwili tree, which they would then ask Lea to bless.

Wailea Resort is one of the most exclusive resort areas in Hawaii. Like Kapalua, Kaanapali, and Waikoloa on the Big Island, Wailea is a planned resort community. In addition to the two great golf courses, the area includes five first-class hotels—including the new Grand Hyatt Wailea—a tennis center, and a shopping complex. Private homes line many of the fairways, and there are also a number of condominium developments.

In 1993, Wailea plans to have a new golf course open. Called the Gold course, it will be a Robert Trent Jones, Jr. design. Called for in the Gold plans are slight modifications to the existing Orange course. The two courses will also share a new clubhouse.

"It's a back-to-basics course," Trent Jones, Jr. said. "The Gold course will be a classic golf course design." In the design process for the Gold course Trent Jones, Jr. studied many of the best courses around the world, and says he incorporated the best features of each.

With much the same landscape to work with as the existing Blue and Orange layouts, and with a master golf course designer at work, the Gold is sure to be a winner.

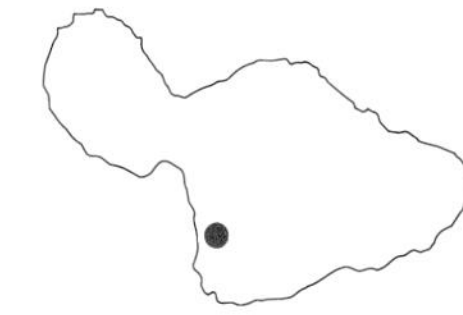

# THE BLUE
## COURSE

*(left) Pretty little sandtraps dot the 15th on the Wailea Blue. You almost don't mind hitting into one.*

The 6,743-yard, par 72 Blue course provides a "restful" challenge in comparison with the Orange. Even so, it has 72 bunkers, four lakes, and natural lava formations to trap poorly hit shots.

There are only two parallel fairways, but generally they are wide open, designed for higher-handicap golfers. The most difficult shots are those from uphill or downhill lies. Colors are everywhere: hibiscus, plumeria, bougainvillea, and hundreds of flowering plants and trees.

The condition of the course is perfect and the overall layout can only help one to score well. Even the wind is not nearly as strong here as on many other Hawaiian coastal courses.

Straight trees are rare on Hawaii's ocean courses. Generally, blustery winds bend trees and golf balls to their will. But at Wailea the trees grow straight, a sign of excellent golfing weather.

*Featured Holes:*

### Hole 6 - 361 Yards Par 4

There is out-of-bounds on the right and an in-range bunker on the left, so from the slightly elevated tee and with the breeze from the left, hit your drive straight down the center. Your second shot, 135 yards from the green, is just as uncomplicated as the drive. Bring your approach shot from the right to hold the ball into the cross breeze. On your way to the next tee you drive through an attractive grove of pink and white plumeria which fill the air with subtle perfume.

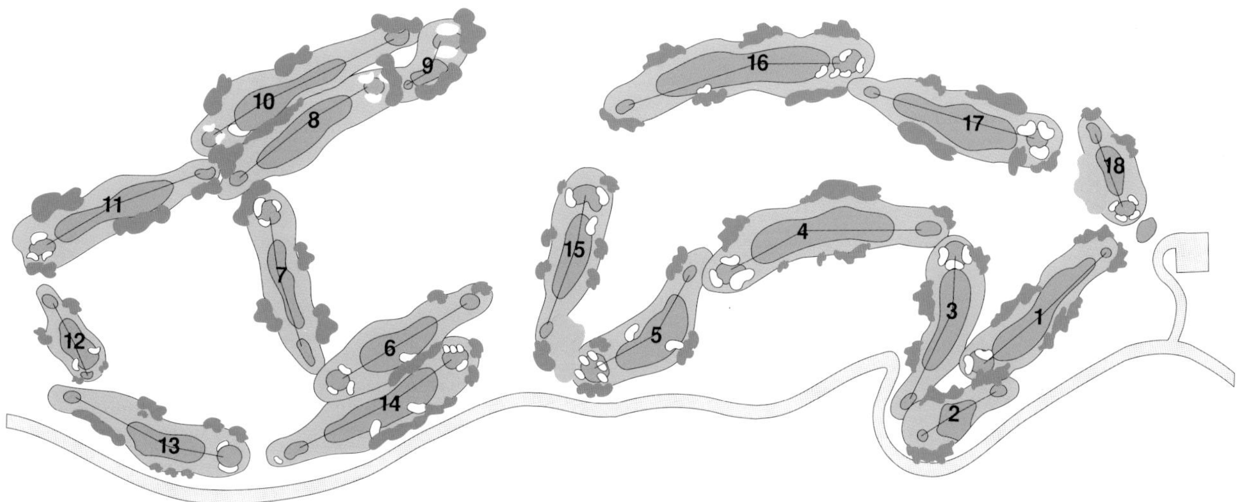

*(above) The 9th green at Wailea Blue, known as one of the finer layouts in the state.*

## Hole 8 - 431 Yards Par 4

There is almost a continuous swale between tee and green on this hole. But it does not present any real problem. There is out-of-bounds on the right and beautiful trees down the left. On the windward right is a kiawe tree that is well out of range. Use that as your target and the wind will help center the shot. You are now about 175 yards from the green, normally a 5-iron. But, because it is all carry, you should bend a 4-iron in from the left. Aiming left will also lessen the menace of the two bunkers.

## Hole 14 - 501 Yards Par 5

In theory, the flag can be reached with two shots. However, let us first concentrate on a good tee shot. There is out-of-bounds right and left. There is also a reachable fairway bunker on the right. The smart thing to do is to hit the driver and balloon it for the buttonwood tree on your right and let it drift in from that direction. The following breeze will help. If you have hit the ball well you should be some 200 yards from this elevated green. There are bunkers everywhere. So pump up a 5-wood and float it straight onto the green.

*(above) The 2nd fairway of the Blue course is lined by condominiums. If your game is off, you can stop in for a cold one!*

## Hole 15 - 360 Yards Par 4

Majestic Haleakala provides a dramatic backdrop to this uphill hole. Both sides of the fairway have out-of-bounds. There is a sizeable water hazard in front and a bunker on the right side of the fairway. The thing to do is hit your drive straight for the kiawe trees, beside the right fairway bunker. The elevated green is 130 yards away. Take notice of which side the flagstick is placed, and whatever you do make certain your ball ends up on the same side.

## Hole 16 - 542 Yards Par 5

This is an interesting tee shot in that you are hitting over a crest, not having the faintest idea of where you are going. Well, here are some facts that might help: the fairway bends right with a slope and there is a bunker and out-of-bounds on the right also. So drive left of center and the gentle trades will protect you from all unseen dangers. Now that you are over the hill, you can see where you are heading. The ideal way onto this green is from the left. Crack a solid 3-wood from 250 yards out and you will find a nice open thoroughfare leading to the putting surface. Finally, a pitch and run. When you've putted out, enjoy the spectacular view of Wailea, the ocean beyond, and the islands of Lanai, Kahoolawe, Molokini, and Molokai.

*The 2nd green at Wailea Blue.*
*Once you've putted out, take a minute to admire one of the most beautiful corners of Hawaii.*

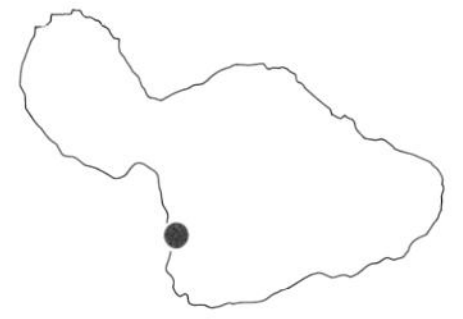

# THE ORANGE COURSE

The wiliwili tree is very rare on Maui today, but one of the few places you'll find it is on the Orange course, its blossoms vivid red in winter. The Orange course is also dotted with a unique hazard, *papohaku*, centuries-old stone walls which have been left intact on eight holes.

The 6,810-yard, par 72 course is a much more demanding track than its Blue neighbor. With trees encroaching onto the narrower fairways, rolling terrain, numerous left and right dog-legs, 40 bunkers, and stone walls, the Orange course calls for rifle-shot accuracy. In fact, accuracy and not length is the key to a successful round of golf.

Some holes have elevated tees and every hole has a sweeping ocean panorama. There is also left a large, natural lava rock formation sitting on the 18th green. It was deposited there by Haleakala, Maui's 10,023-foot dormant volcano.

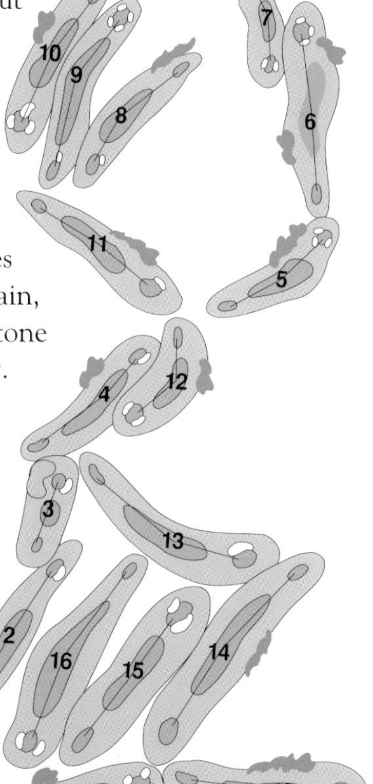


*(left) The Orange course, 4th tee. A 423-yard par four: aim straight at Molokai in the distance.*

*(above) Roughly 150 yards from the green on the 8th you'll encounter one of the old Hawaiian lava stone walls which have been left intact on the Orange course.*

*Featured Holes:*

## Hole 4 - 423 Yards Par 4

Try not to be mesmerized by the magnificent scenery on your backswing. Hit your driver straight at the buttonwood tree on your right. The breeze should bring your ball in from the right, positioning it in the middle of the fairway, which sports a number of wiliwili trees. You are now some 160 yards from the green, which is eye level, but there is a swale in front. There is only one bunker at the right front to trouble you. The rest of the contoured green is protected by grassy slopes. Take one more club than you think for your second shot.

## Hole 5 - 392 Yards Par 4

You are off to the ocean, downhill. Aim a 2-iron at the buttonwood trees. The breeze is coming in from the right. Whatever you do, don't stray too far left, you'll be in diabolical trouble. A strong 7-iron second shot will put you on the middle of this green. To encourage you to hit straight, there is an array of bunkers along the right side, a lava bed and kiawe trees on the left. Having achieved a satisfactory result with your 7-iron shot, spend a few seconds and look at an interesting piece of Hawaiian history nearby. There is an ancient meeting place and the remains of a wall.

*(above) A 206-yard par three, the 17th typifies both Wailea courses: beautiful views and exquisitely maintained layouts.*

## Hole 10 - 531 Yards Par 5

A drive holding into the side breeze down the center will place your ball in a perfect position. On your way to the ball it is advisable to pick a target on the skyline for your next shot. This fairway is undulating and there is a hollow where the good drive usually lands from which the green cannot be seen. Aiming at your predetermined target, use a healthy 3-wood, holding it against the left-hand breeze. Try not to hit this shot too high. You should have now nestled into another gentle hollow. There are two bunkers on the left and one on the right guarding this rather large green.

## Hole 18 - 426 Yards Par 4

It doesn't matter whether you have heard this hole described as "famous" or "infamous," the description is right on both counts. There is no evident fairway, just a narrow, tree-lined avenue. The fairway, veering to the left, is cunningly concealed over the brow of a hill. Take a deep breath, muster up your best swash-buckling attitude, and hit your driver down the right side. Well, now, like a mirage ahead and below is the green, surrounded by beautiful vegetation. A soft 7-iron sneaking in from the right will relieve the tension of the previous shot. Try not to land short, but just comfortably on the putting surface. In the middle of the green is a lava formation which was used by the ancient Hawaiians as a cooking site. This is probably the only golf course on this planet that has 19th hole facilities in the middle of the 18th green!

ISLAND OF

# HAWAII

The Big Island of Hawaii was the first to be inhabited by Polynesian settlers (A.D. 600 to 700), yet geologically it is the youngest of the islands, barely a million years old.

It is the most dramatic of the Hawaiian chain, with its parched deserts, glistening black sand beaches, and red lava flows from Kilauea Volcano – the mythological home of the fire goddess Pele.

Sometimes called the Orchid Island for the wild purple blossoms that grace the roadsides of Puna and Hilo, and also for the commercial orchid production which has sprung up in recent years, the Big Island is a wondrous combination of snow-covered mountains, lush valleys where waterfalls break through rock faces, dozens of glorious white sand beaches, and a stretch of sunny coastline 90 miles long on the Kona side of the island.

The Big Island, a rough diamond in shape, dwarfs the other islands at 4,038 square miles. It continues to grow every day as lava spills dramatically into the ocean.

*An other-worldly glow occurs where the molten lava meets the sea*

# HILO MUNICIPAL
## GOLF COURSE

*(left) Hilo municipal is a very green course due to frequent rainfall. Here the 342-yard par four 7th.*

The island of Hawaii, commonly referred to as the Big Island, is larger than all of the other Hawaiian Islands combined. However, it possesses only 10 percent of the state's population, which amounts to roughly 100,000 people. The Big Island is a dynamic landscape which continues to grow as the active volcano Kilauea spews lava into the ocean off the southern shore.

Located on the eastern coast of the island, the city of Hilo is home to the island's only publicly-owned golf course, the Hilo Municipal Golf Course. It is basically a flat layout, which opened for play in 1951. One of the greater assets of the 18-hole par 71 course is that it sits with a perfect view of beautiful Hilo Bay on one side, and the towering Mauna Kea—the world's tallest mountain if measured from its ocean base—on the other.

Offering more than 6,000 yards of play from the back tees, Hilo municipal's design consists of a playable blend of pars, with par fours consuming 50 percent of the course. Designed by Willard G. Wilkinson, the course has no sand at all. But because of its location on the wet side of the Big Island, Hilo municipal is subject to frequent rains. After a heavy rainfall play is slow, and your yardage per hit is reduced. Fairways are occasionally soggy.

Because of the course's proximity to Hilo and the fact that a round of golf is inexpensive, it is an extremely popular course. Since its first days, the Hilo Municipal Golf Course has been a favorite of Big Island residents and today there are more than 92,000 rounds of golf played on it annually.

The past three years have seen a significant increase in tourism on the island. Most of this activity has focused on the new resort developments along the sunny Kohala coast and the ever-popular town of Kona which offers some of the best big game fishing in the world.

And while Hilo is not a major stopping point for visitors, it certainly has charms of its own to offer. Plus, it is one of the best access points to Kilauea Volcano, an hour's drive away. And on a sunny day, a round of golf at Hilo municipal can be quite relaxing indeed.

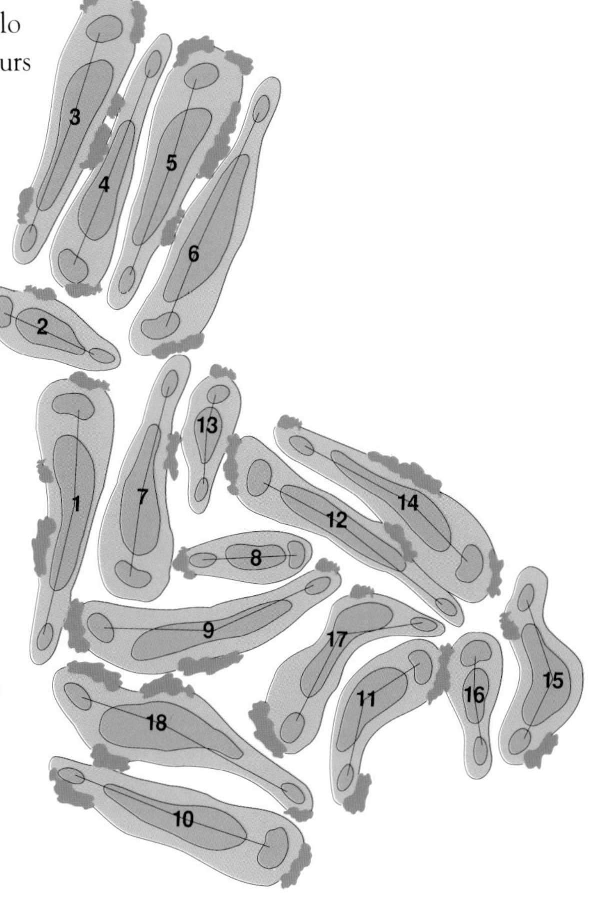

# KONA
## COUNTRY CLUB

Ocean and mountain vistas set off Keauhou Bay, 14 miles south of the Keahole Airport, along the Kona Coast. Here you'll find 27 holes of beautiful golf at the Kona Country Club, all of it adjacent to some of the world's best big-game fishing.

*(left) Plenty of lava, a lake, some sand, just the right sprinkling of palm trees, and a distractingly gorgeous view make the Mauka 7th at Kona a fun hole to play.*

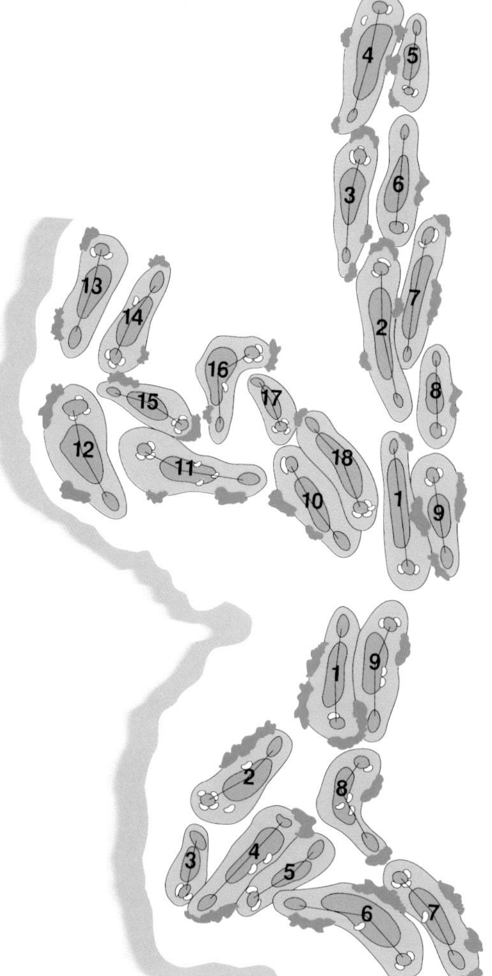


Billy Bell designed the course, some of which skirts the ocean before heading up into hills of lava, where it offers scenic ocean panoramas from tree-lined fairways.

Big, fast, rolling greens with a variety of pin placements, give any golfer a challenge, and the par threes are as demanding as you will find anywhere. Fortunately, the course is protected from the sometimes brutal trade winds by the mountains.

This is an interesting area, where some of the first Polynesian explorers settled, attracted by the good fishing, temperate climate, and abundant vegetation.

Their ancient, walled City of Refuge (where outcasts were granted sanctuary) is now a historic monument, and the nearby village of Kailua-Kona was home to the first missionaries of these islands.

Not too far from here, at Kealakekua Bay, on February 4, 1788, Captain James Cook died in a skirmish with the Hawaiians. A bronze plaque, often awash by waves, marks the exact spot where Cook fell.

*(above) The 3rd tee at Kona, looking at the ocean.*

*Featured Holes:*

## OCEAN FRONT NINE

### Hole 2 - 500 Yards Par 5

An honest driving hole, so aim your driver down the center of a well-defined fairway. You now repeat that shot, only with a 3-wood, because the green is still not visible. The decision on how to make five can only be made when you have reached your second. Now for the business end of this hole. You are confronted with a good-looking target, the ocean as a backdrop, palm trees, and a contoured, well-bunkered green. There is no advice needed here for your third. Play it as you see it, but remember the slope from back to front is negated by the grain going with the ball.

## OCEAN BACK NINE

### Hole 10 - 350 Yards Par 4 (Hole 1 on the Ocean Back)

A 150-foot-deep grassy gully separates the tee and the green on this hole. There is no run on your drive. What you carry is what you get. On the right there is a lava garden and a heavily wooded area down the left, so drop your driver down the middle as far as you can. Before you leave the tee take a fix on the pin placement, as you will not be able to see the flag or green from down in the valley. As a confirmation of green position, aim for the left of the two palms you can see on the skyline. A wedge tossed well up will be the most successful stroke to this fairly large green.

*(above) The colorful 10th green, with the Kona Surf Resort in the background.*

## Hole 13 - 420 Yards Par 4

If nothing else this hole has been suitably numbered. The tee mound is built on a small peninsula. Your shot goes over a natural inlet, a lava bed, fishermen on the in-between rocks, and a blow hole. Talk about water hazards! Depending on the conditions of the day, this water hazard can go from horizontal to a 60-foot vertical spray of water. Don't let all this melt your concentration. Forget it and take aim at the green. Put your head down and some steam into your drive straight down the center, disregarding the out-of-bounds on your left. You now have to hop from one plateau to another, where the green is situated. Hit a 4-wood coming from the left with the wind, and it should put a smile on your face.

# MAUKA NINE

## Hole 7 - 440 Yards Par 4

Before taking any club out, give your camera an airing on this hole. From this elevated tee you look down a fairway bordered by lava beds, with some coconut palms. There is water on your right and there are fairway bunkers. Take your 3-wood and charge it straight for the right-hand bunker. The breeze and the slope compensate for one another, and your target area is probably the narrowest part of the fairway. Now a shot for those who have a flair for the dramatic. The green has lava left, lava right, lava back, and water in front. You now have a cash and carry situation: cash in on your talent with a 6-iron and carry all the way to the green. There is absolutely no margin for error.

*Fronting the 3rd hole of the Ocean course is a rocky Pacific inlet. Try not to become a spectator here.*

# MAUNA KEA

The Mauna Kea course was designed by Robert Trent Jones, Sr. and opened for play in 1964. It was immediately branded a savagely tough layout from the championship tees.

It was a masterpiece, carved from an ancient lava bed beside the ocean, and it became the blueprint for all other Hawaiian courses to follow on similar terrain.

The resort was named after Mauna Kea — "White Mountain" — an occasionally snow-dusted volcanic peak, which at 13,784 feet, is the scenic fulcrum from the velvety green fairways.

It was this spot on the Kohala coast that Laurance Rockefeller selected for one of the world's great luxury resort hotels, the Mauna Kea Beach Hotel. Sitting beside Kaunaoa Bay, it has an ideal beach and perfect weather.

*(left) The famous 3rd of Mauna Kea. Golfers must shoot 210 yards of Pacific carry to finish this magnificent hole in par.*

Rockefeller wanted a golf course, but there was one problem: the lava. He asked Trent Jones to fly to Hawaii to take a look. Rockefeller asked, "Well, Trent, can you build a golf course on this?"

Jones picked up two chunks of lava and crashed them together with his hands. The pieces crumbled and fell on the ground.

"If I can break this stuff with my hands," Jones replied, "we'll have no trouble with our machinery. You've got your course."

The most dramatic hole is the 3rd, which plays from a tee on one lava rock over an inlet of the bay to a green on another lava rock 210 yards away. Jones had originally placed a back tee with a carry of some 250 yards over the Pacific. It was abandoned after Gary Player failed to clear the water in a practice round for a 72-hole televised match in 1964.

The 3rd green carries the Trent Jones trademark of sharp borrows and lightning speed, especially from the back-right towards the ocean. Fortunately, not every hole is as unforgiving after a mis-hit shot.

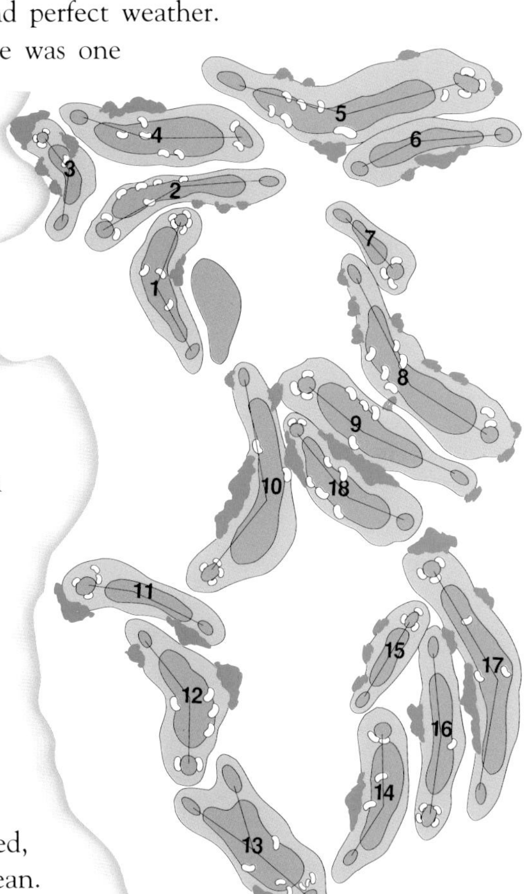


Even so, the captivating course, with no lakes and few level lies, remains a tough hombre from the back tees. To beat the course you have to drive the ball well, keeping it in play and paying particular attention to your putting.

*(above) Downhill all the way to the 11th green. From start to finish, Mauna Kea is a Trent Jones, Sr. delight.*

Featured Holes:

## Hole 3 - 210 Yards Par 3

This is one of the most famous par threes in world golf, the showcase hole at Mauna Kea. Your tee shot has to carry the ocean, but many, fearful of splashing their balls into the Pacific and among the huge manta rays that frequent this inlet, hit to the right and are then faced with a desperate scramble to salvage a par.

Have a go. It's a big green, 58 yards from the front to the back, but with three levels. Carefully study the grain.

## Hole 5 - 593 Yards Par 5

This is a genuine three-shot par five. Not only is it a long par five, but the third shot is to an elevated green, so once again be careful with your club selection. Your tee shot should be aimed to the right plateau on the fairway, or else hit a draw shot. A ball hit with the driver to the middle of this fairway will give you a sloping lie.

Try to hit your second shot well enough to reach the banyan trees on the right-hand side of the fairway. There's a sprinkler in the rough there which lets you know you are 149 yards from the green. The grain on the green runs towards the ocean, so once again it is very slick from back to front.

*(above) You've got plenty of fairway but also plenty of wind. The green is guarded by bunkers and in the distance a dormant volcano looms. Above all, stay calm.*

## Hole 16 - 422 Yards Par 4

Aim your tee shot at the left side of the fairway, because the wind often drifts the ball to the right, and from there a cluster of palm trees can block your second shot to the green.

Be careful with your second shot. The green is well-guarded by bunkers and at the back slopes away from the direction of your approach shot. There is a 150-yard marker just past the palm trees, but you are more likely to be hitting from a sprinkler on the left, 178 yards from the front edge of the green.

## Hole 18 - 428 Yards Par 4

The trick on this final hole is to aim your tee shot towards the hotel elevator. It looks as though you are aiming at trees, but the wind off the ocean will drift your ball to the center of the fairway. If you don't believe me and aim down the center of the fairway, I'll have the last laugh when I see you digging your ball out from volcanic rock and trees. Your second shot, with several yardages on sprinklers to assist your club selection from the top of the hill, should be directed at the right half of the green. A ball hit to the left will roll back off the front of the green.

*An aerial view of holes 2, 3, and 4 shows the terrain from which the Mauna Kea course was wrought, as well as its setting against the sparkling Pacific.*

# MAUNA LANI
## RESORT

*(left) The 17th at Mauna Lani is a short 116-yard par three with lava, lava, and more lava. Oh, and a touch of sand for good measure.*

The molten rock which once flowed down to the Kohala Coast at Mauna Lani hardened into an immense bed of black, craggy, twisted, surreal shapes.

It remained untouched until designer Ray Cain and builder Homer Flint came together to create a 6,750-yard, par 72 layout, the fairways of which look like green ribbons smoothed across the moon's surface, forming lush paths to the blue Pacific.

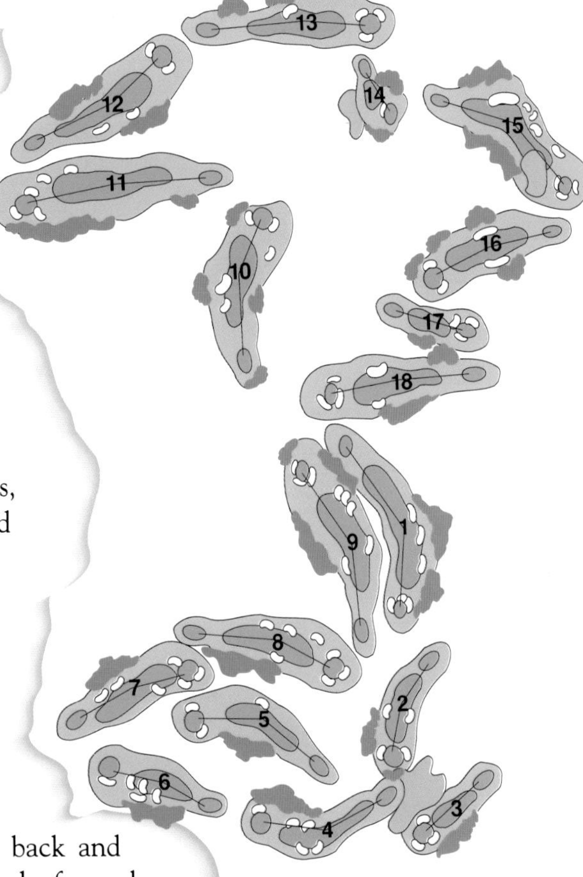


At some points on the course, named after Francis H. I'i Brown, the original owner of the land and one of Hawaii's most famous sporting figures, the lava rises 100 feet above the fairways. Even so, Flint's work appears more the result of a scalpel than a bulldozer.

The strikingly beautiful par three 6th hole, across the ocean, is Mauna Lani's answer to Mauna Kea's 3rd, or Cypress Point's 16th.

There are five sets of tees on most holes, and when played from the regular 6,206-yard tees, it is a course where a 20 handicapper can marvel at the scenery and break 90 at the same time.

With three lakes, 85 bunkers, and 175 coconut trees—not forgetting the lava—Mauna Lani has enough difficulty to keep your mind on golf.

Director of golf Jerry Johnston says, "Mauna Lani doesn't particularly break your back and (the course) is good for women. But I'm tired of people coming in and telling me what a great facility this is. After 30 years in the business I'm used to complaints!"

Remember when playing the course you'll often encounter a 10-knot "Kona wind." This is exactly the opposite of the prevailing tradewinds which blow at a steady 25 knots.

*(above) One of the most photographed holes in golf, the 6th at Mauna Lani asks only a little water carry—roughly 200 yards. Don't let it psyche you out.*

*Featured Holes:*

## Hole 5 - 410 Yards Par 4

The sight confronting you consists mainly of two colors, black and green. Stick with the green. While trying to bend your shot into the left-hand Kona wind, aim for the right-hand bunkers with your driver. From this point, keep your 7-iron against the breeze and try to bull's-eye this green that has both bunkers and lava on guard.

## Hole 6 - 199 Yards Par 3

Both the tee and green are 60 feet above sea level, and in between is the Pacific Ocean washing the lava cliffs. The more-than-spacious green is guarded by five large bunkers. The spectacular vision before you is a gorgeous canvas of black, blue, and green, making the 6th one of Hawaii's most photographed holes. Between the 6th green and the 7th tee there are still remains of some fishermen's cottages or shelters built in the 1600s.

*(above) The 14th pin is situated between two lava - bed lakes.*

## Hole 15 - 501 Yards Par 5

This par five dog-leg angles some 45 degrees to the right, but is not your concern with the tee shot. Just make the bend by aiming your driver at the last three bunkers on the left, bending your shot to hold it into the right-hand breeze. Try not to be shaken by the amount of lava around you. Your second shot is from a plateau on the bend. From this position you have a grand view of what is expected of you: miss the lava, water and bunkers front and back – that's the right side. The left side has only two giant bunkers short and one at the back of the green. What is needed is common sense. Hit a 3-wood to finish short of the green and a touch left of center. Now you've got it made, just a toss up and onto this wide but shallow green.

## Hole 17 - 136 Yards Par 3

This is a beauty. Standing on the elevated tee you are confronted with an emerald green oasis in a black desert of lava. The 17th at Mauna Lani is another of the most photographed holes in Hawaii. There are accómmodating bunkers around the rear and one large bunker directly in front. Rising out of this bed of sand is a monolith of lava. I would like to think that this is a salute to Homer Flint, a true percipient and the builder of this fine layout. Now, to cap off all the beauty, play an 8-iron just right of center and get yourself a birdie.

*An aerial shot of Mauna Lani tells the story: green ribbons laid out on a canvas of black lava.*

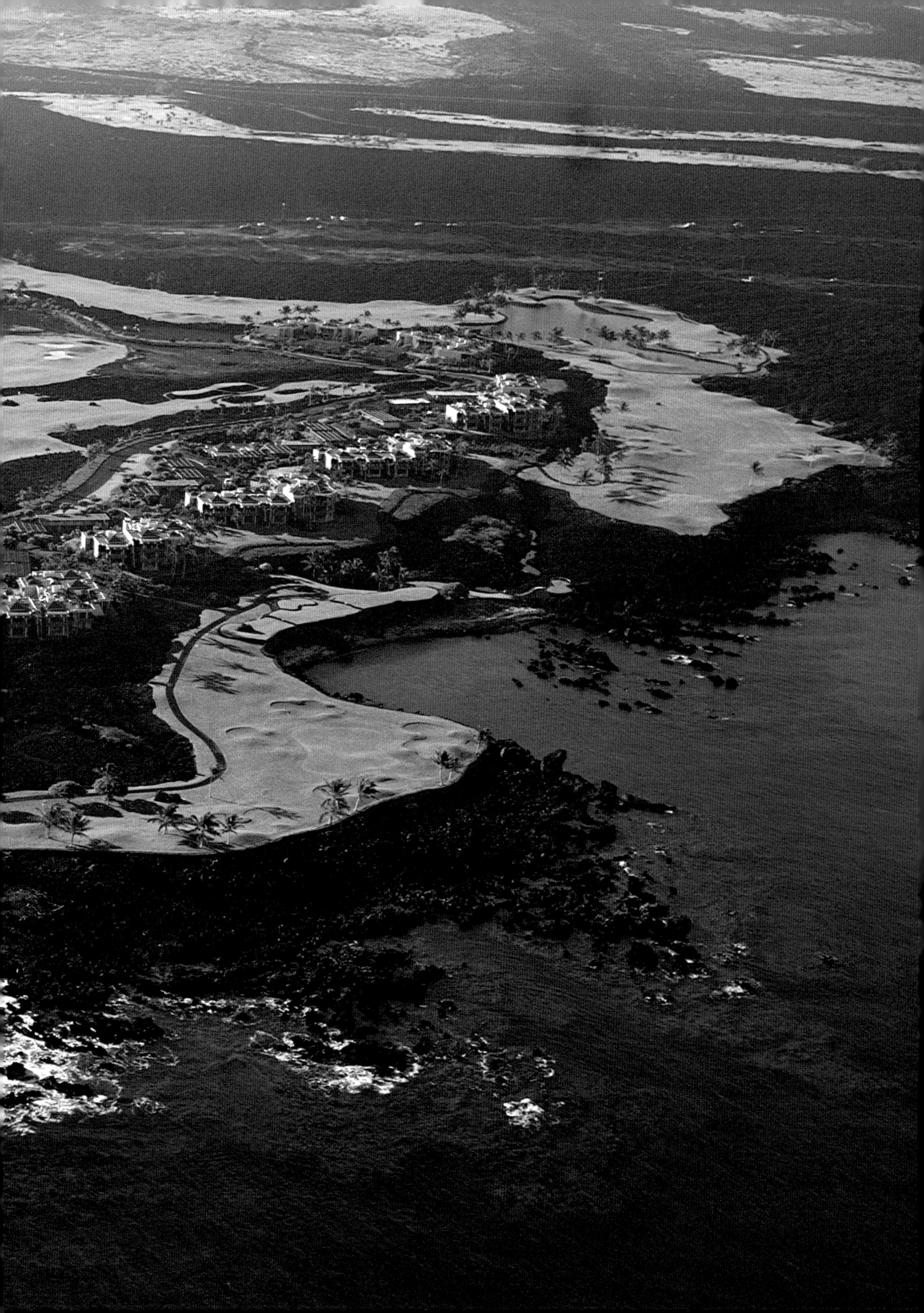

# VOLCANO
## GOLF AND COUNTRY CLUB

Volcano Golf and Country Club, 4,000 feet above sea level, was once a large pasture on the slopes of majestic Mauna Loa mountain. It was called Keahou Ranch, owned and operated by Mr. W. A. Shipman.

On a summer day in 1922, his grandson, Roy C. Blackshear, had a wild idea to carve out a hole to play some golf. He received permission from his grandfather and used sand to smooth out the putting surface, choosing an old tomato can for the hole.

After one year of playing and mastering the hole, Mr. Blackshear and his golfing partner, Mr. Goff, decided to "build" two more holes. A single strand of barbed wire encircled each green to keep all the cattle from romping on and fertilizing them.

Word spread fast and more friends came over to challenge their mini golf course.

By 1928, the first nine was completed along with the first clubhouse (a shack on stilts) to accommodate the many golfing friends and foes that Mr. Blackshear had amassed!

*(below) The 1st green at Volcano. A good layout in a fascinating area.*

Mrs. Laura Kennedy, a good friend of Mr. Blackshear, kindly donated the funds required to build the second nine, which was completed in the early 1940s. The course grew in popularity so quickly that a membership was finally established and, to this day, continues to grow.

Every year in March, the Founder's "Tomato Can" Golf Tournament is held for the members in memory of Roy C. Blackshear.

The course is almost next door to Kilauea crater, the world's most active volcano. At this altitude you have gained almost 10 yards on your distance—one full club. The 150-yard markers are indicated by beautiful camellia bushes.

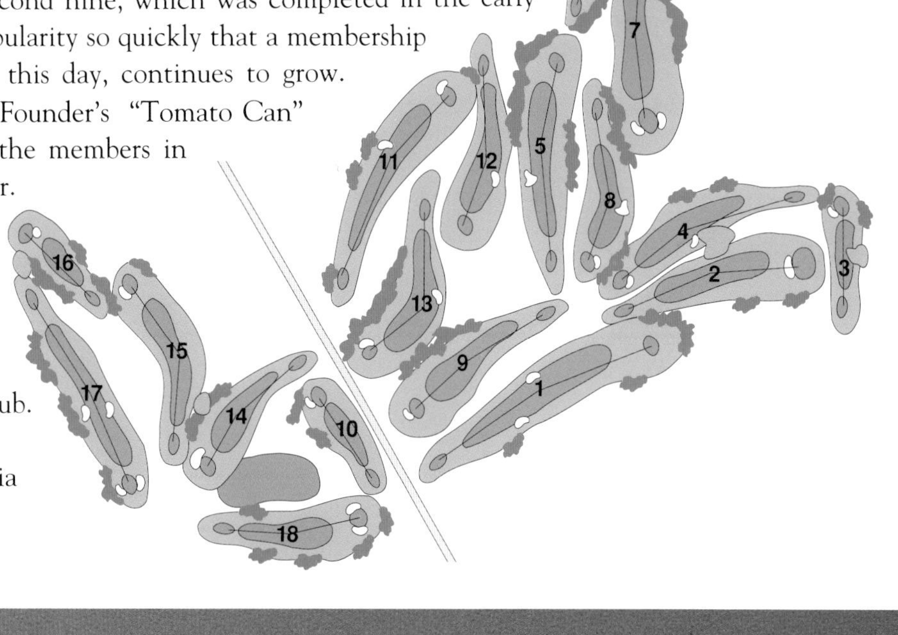

# WAIKOLOA RESORT

There are two courses built on black lava beside the ocean at Waikoloa, 17 miles north of Keahole (Kona) Airport on the famed Kohala Coast, and another located eight miles into the foothills at Waikoloa Village.

The first, designed by Robert Trent Jones, Jr., opened in 1981, and a new course, designed by Tom Weiskopf and Jay Morrish, the King's Course, opened in the spring of 1990.

Both courses take the golfer through a large slice of Hawaiian history. The Jones course—the Beach—has historic caves, petroglyph fields, and ancient lava flows, all part of the 6,605-yard layout.

There are 75 crushed-coral bunkers, three lakes, tight fairways and, with the lava legacy of the 13,784-foot-high Mauna Kea volcano bordering every hole, players will have plenty to think about during a round, with accuracy rather than distance the key thought.

Like its neighbors, Mauna Lani and Mauna Kea, the new King's Course offers spectacular scenery with the fairways, like green ribbons, winding between the huge black lava flows.

It always seems astonishing that such spectacularly scenic golf can be coaxed from a moonscape-type lava coastline.

The Waikoloa area encompasses quite a bit of land, running from the foothills of Mauna Kea down to the beach. There are two hotels—the Royal Waikoloan and the Hyatt Regency Waikoloa—and some condominium developments at the water's edge. And up in the foothills, Waikoloa Village boasts its own condos and golf course, another Robert Trent Jones, Jr. design.

*(left) The Hyatt Regency Waikoloa hotel offers guests a unique experience in hotel accommodations. It is truly a fantasy resort.*

# THE BEACH
## COURSE

The Beach Course, like most other layouts on the Kohala Coast, can provide a challenge to the accomplished golfer. On the same token, it can be a real workout for the duffer. The out-of-bounds is more often than not a lava field, in which a lost ball can be forgotten. Even if you're lucky enough to find it, it's going to be scarred deeply from its encounter with the sharp lava.

*(left) Water awaits the errant shot on the 4th at Waikoloa Beach, a 126-yard par three.*

Located next to the Hyatt Regency Waikoloa and the Royal Waikoloan hotels, the Beach Course is best played with an early morning tee-time. The afternoon heat in the lava rocks can be sweltering, and the winds tend to pick up later in the day as well.

It is a beautiful course, with holes 13 and 14 bordered by the Pacific Ocean.

*Featured Holes:*

### Hole 4 - 126 Yards Par 3

A picturesque hole with dark lava in front, along the left and at the back, broken up by a row of palms at the back. A water hole both right and front and bunkers, suggests only one thing more: you need a 7-iron shot to be on the putting surface.

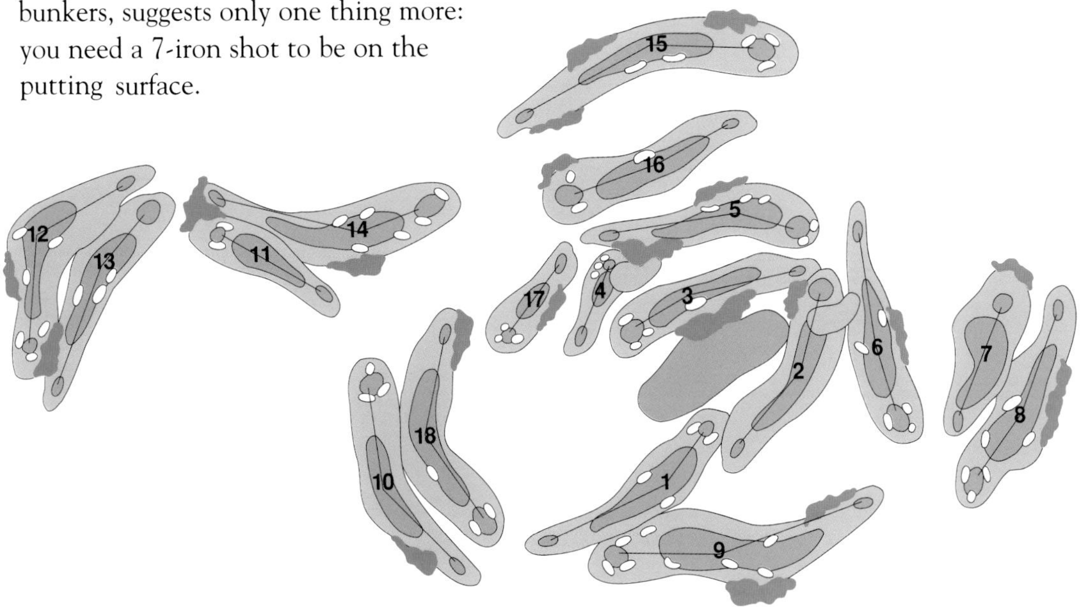

*(above) The 5th tee of the Beach course asks only a short lava carry down to a wide fairway.*

## Hole 6 - 387 Yards Par 4

The holiday is over. The first five holes have been relatively uneventful, but this is the first hole into the tradewinds. From possibly the highest point of this course you are confronted with playing a slight right-to-left tee shot with your driver, making sure you carry the water hazard 150 yards from the tee. You should divide the distance between the two driveable bunkers right and left of the fairway. The sole palm tree right of center is your target. On the left side of the fairway is a lava bed that you should be warned about, because not only would you get an impossible lie, but there are carvings there that warn you to be careful. Before you leave the tee, be sure you have determined whether the pin is positioned in the front or at the back of the green. For your second shot, punch a 6-iron to the green, remembering the two bunkers on the left and the one on the right. This second shot is a little easier for the right-hander as the ball is above the stance. Across the middle of this green is a ridge giving you a downhill putt to the front and the back, so make sure you are on the same half of the green as the hole.

## Hole 12 - 492 Yards Par 5

From this tee you now head for the Pacific. However, everything is not what it seems. With the contouring of the fairway and the positioning of bunkers, you

*(above) Yawning bunkers guard the 5th green.*

can be tricked into thinking that the fairway veers right. In fact, it is quite the opposite. So direct your driver to barely miss the nearest left-hand bunker and you will finish near the center of the fairway. Now, if you think and play to the right, where there is plenty of room, you have added several clubs to this already long, into-the-wind hole. If you have played the ideal tee shot, you now have a choice of getting everything out of a 3-wood to carry from one plateau to the next, with lava and valley in between, or a more conservative shot and play a full 3-iron left of center to allow your short third shot to run up the neck of this widening green. Should you be visiting during the early part of the year, you could be distracted by the humpback whales passing only 200 yards offshore, doing their thing while you are trying to do yours, which is to putt out successfully.

## Hole 18 - 410 Yards Par 4

With the breeze head on, aim your drive straight at the bunker with your 2-wood. The bunker is sited between lava on the right and out-of-bounds on the left. Do not aim at the catamaran with the red sails in the background, as it might have changed position by the time you get to play this great finishing hole. For your second shot, hit your 4-iron just right and the trades will bring your ball back to this long and narrow green, which is adequately guarded by bunkers on both sides. The shape of this green is almost that of an hourglass with a waist of only about 20 feet.

# THE KING'S COURSE

The new King's Course at Waikoloa is destined to be the standard measure for new golf courses built in Hawaii.

The 7,064-yard, par 72 layout features six major lakes, about 70 bunkers ranging from several small pot bunkers to some 60 to 70 feet long, creative use of undulations and mounding, and fairways of Tifton 328 Bermuda grass and greens of TIF-Dwarf.

Respect for wind conditions led designers Tom Weiskopf and Jay Morrish to create generous fairway widths with rough of moderate height. Each of the four par five holes, and each of the par three holes plays into a different wind condition.

This maintains the integrity of their lengths, regardless of wind conditions. The scratch or low handicap player may be able to reach three of the four par fives in two strokes, but the longest hole will seldom be reached in two. Each par three will need a different iron.

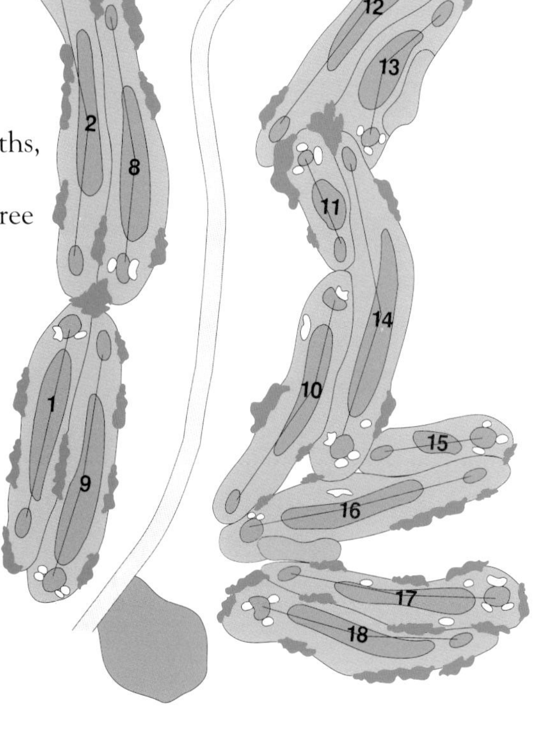


*(left) The green of the 501-yard par five 18th on the King's course is overlooked by the clubhouse. Par out and walk in with your head held high.*

*(above) A windy day, massive lava rocks, and a splash of sand … classic King's.*

*Featured Holes:*

## Hole 5 - 327 Yards Par 4

This is a straightaway hole with lava on the right, lava outcrops on the left and bunkers right and left. If that isn't enough, the bunker on the left runs nearly half the length of the fairway with two lava outcrops in it. The sand stretches for 150 yards! The accuracy of your drive is very important, because the shorter your second shot the better to this multi-level green. And, if you are not careful, you could spend some time here — putting.

## Hole 10 - 453 Yards Par 4

The lava continues down the left side and is sprinkled about on the right. The bunkers that guard the left side are deep, making it almost impossible for the hapless victim to reach the green, so try not to veer off center. A 6-iron second shot is needed to carry the dead ground between you and the target. It is best to come in from the right, using the shape of the green, and away from the deep bunkers on the right.

*(above) The 14th is a 601-yard par five monster, requiring both length and accuracy to avoid the fairway hazards.*

## Hole 14 - 591 Yards Par 5

A continuous carpet of lava runs down the left side, and the right side is sprinkled with lava in between contours. Make full use of the breeze coming in from the right by aiming your drive right of center. Dog-legging slightly to the right, this fairway is bunker-free, though it sports the usual undulations. Instead of sand traps there are numerous lava mounds reaching a height of more than eight feet. This is a wonderful example of making full use of the natural materials and formations. Now, pound a 3-wood second shot at the right-hand bunker, followed up by a solid wedge, but not too high. Watch out for the bunker at the rear of the green.

## Hole 18 - 501 Yards Par 5

A beautiful finishing hole. Both the prevailing tradewinds and the dog-leg go right. Your tee shot must be aimed at the second bunker, past the four lava outcrops on the left side, leaning the ball gently to the right. Follow this with at least a strong mid-iron, if not a club more, onto a plateau, ready to attack the last green which has bunkers that are yawning, just waiting for you to arrive. A wedge should infiltrate the green without disturbing any of the traps.

*A clear day on the Kohala coast, Mauna Kea mountain in the background. Here Waikoloa King's 5th green.*

# THE VILLAGE
## COURSE

Waikoloa Village Golf Course, also designed by Robert Trent Jones, Jr., is located about eight miles away from the two courses at Waikoloa Beach.

*(left) A 200-yard par three at the Village course. Aim directly at the Pacific Ocean.*

By comparison to the layouts near the ocean, the Village's 6,687-yard, par 72 course has more hills (1,000 feet above sea level), with elevated greens and tees, numerous dog-legs, and strategically placed fairway and green-side bunkers.

With its sage and mesquite trees, the tract closely resembles a California high desert course. There are also palms, Norfolk pines, kiawe, ironwood, and eucalyptus trees.

The course is overlooked by both Mauna Loa and Mauna Kea mountains. It, in turn, looks over the north and south Kohala coasts, the Pacific Ocean, and the island of Maui in the distance.

*Featured Hole:*

## Hole 5 - 399 Yards Par 4

This hole is mean and honest at the same time. It is the hardest hole on the course. It is against the tradewinds, a real test of who is boss. There is a kiawe tree right of center, not reachable, but aim at it and try, with a bit of right-to-left, and keep the ball quail high. You should then be 175-180 yards out from a green that has no run up to it. Under normal circumstances a well-hit 5- or 4-iron would be required—forget it! To carry on to this green you have to light the fuse of a 2-iron. Be careful of the grain when you putt.

# List of Golf Courses

## Island of Kauai

**Kauai Lagoons Golf & Racquet Club, Kiele Course**
Kalapaki Beach, Lihue, Hawaii 96766 • (808) 245-5050
Resort • 18 Holes • Par 72
Green Fees: $65 - $125 • Golf Carts: included (mandatory)
Open daily 6:30 a.m. - 6:00 p.m. • Tee times: required

**Kauai Lagoons Golf & Racquet Club, Lagoons Course**
Kalapaki Beach, Lihue, Hawaii 96766 • (808) 245-5050
Resort • 18 Holes • Par 72
Green Fees: $45 - $85 • Golf Carts: included (mandatory)
Open daily 6:30 a.m. - 6:00 p.m. • Tee times: required

**Kiahuna Golf Club**
2545 Kiahuna Plantation Drive, Koloa, Hawaii 96756 • (808) 742-9595
Resort • 18 Holes • Par 70
Green Fees: $38 - $75 • Golf Carts: included (mandatory)
Open daily 7:00 a.m. - sunset • Tee times: advised

**Kukuiolono Golf Course**
P.O. Box 1031, Kalaheo, Hawaii 96741 • (808) 332-9151
Public • 9 Holes • Par 36
Green Fees: $5 • Golf Carts: $5 (optional)
Open daily 6:30 a.m. - 4:30 p.m. • Tee times: not required

**Princeville Resort Kauai Makai Course**
P.O. Box 3040, Princeville, Hawaii 96722 • (808) 826-3580
Resort • 27 Holes • Par 72
Green Fees: $60 - $85 • Golf Carts: included (mandatory)
Open daily 7:00 a.m. - 6:30 p.m. • Tee times: preferred

**Princeville Resort Kauai Prince Course**
P.O. Box 3040, Princeville, Hawaii 96722 • (808) 826-3240
Resort • 18 Holes • Par 72
Green Fees: $60 - $85 • Golf Carts: included (mandatory)
Open daily 7:00 a.m. - 6:00 p.m. • Tee times: preferred

**Wailua Municipal Golf Course**
P.O. Box 1017, Kapaa, Hawaii 96746 • (808) 245-8092
Municipal • 18 Holes • Par 72
Green Fees: $10 - $11 • Golf Carts: $12 (optional)
Open daily 7:30 a.m. - 6:30 p.m. • Tee times: preferred

## Island of Oahu

**Ala Wai Municipal Golf Course**
404 Kapahulu Ave., Honolulu, Hawaii 96815 • (808)296-4653
Municipal • 18 Holes • Par 70
Green Fees: $8 - $20 • Golf Carts: $11 (optional)
Open daily 6:00 a.m. - 6:00 p.m.
Tee times: required one week in advance

**Barbers Point Golf Course**
NAS Barbers Point, Hawaii 96862 • (808) 682-3088
Military • 18 Holes • Par 72
Green Fees: $12 public (military guest) • Golf Carts: $6 (optional)
Open daily 6:30 a.m. - 6:30 p.m. • Tee times: required weekends only

**Bayview Golf Course**
45-285 Kaneohe Bay Dr., Kaneohe, Hawaii 96744 • (808) 247-0451
Public • 18 Holes • Par 54 (Par 3 Course)
Green Fees: $5 • Golf Carts: not available
Open daily 7:30 a.m. - 9:00 p.m. • Tee times: not required

**Hawaii Country Club**
P.O. Box 966, Wahiawa, Hawaii 96786 (808) 621-5654
Public • 18 Holes • Par 72
Green Fees: $21 - $60 • Golf Carts: included
Open daily sunrise to sunset • Tee times: required

**Hawaii Kai Championship Golf Course**
8902 Kalanianaole Hwy., Honolulu, Hawaii 96825 • (808) 395-2358
Public • 18 Holes • Par 72
Green Fees: $33 - $70 • Golf Carts: included (mandatory)
Open daily 6:30 a.m. - 6:00 p.m.
Tee times: required one week in advance

**Hawaii Kai Executive Golf Course**
8902 Kalanianaole Hwy., Honolulu, Hawaii 96825 • (808)395-2358
Public • 18 Holes • Par 55 (Par 3 Course)
Green Fees: $11.50 • Golf Carts: $8.00 (optional)
Open daily 6:30 a.m. - 6:00 p.m.
Tee times: required one week in advance

**Hickam Mamala Bay Golf Course**
Bldg. 3572, Hickam AFB, Hawaii 96853 • (808) 449-6490
Military • 18 Holes • Par 72
Green Fees: $20 public (military guest)
Golf Carts: $5 per person (optional)
Open daily 6:00 a.m. - 6:30 p.m. • Tee times: required

**Hickam Par-Three Golf Course**
Bldg. 2105, Hickam AFB, Hawaii 96853 • (808) 449-2093
Military • 9 Holes • Par 27
Green Fees: $2 - $3 (military guest) • Golf Carts: not available
Open daily 7:00 a.m. - 10:00 p.m. • Tee times: required

**Honolulu Country Club**
1690 Ala Puumalu St., Honolulu, Hawaii 96818 • (808) 833-4541
Private • 18 Holes • Par 72
Green Fees: vary (guests must be sponsored by a member)
Golf Carts: $18 (mandatory during specific times)
Open daily 7:00 a.m. - sunset • Tee times: required

**Kahuku Golf Course**
P.O. Box 517, Kahuku, Hawaii 96731 • (808) 293-5842
Municipal • 9 Holes • Par 35
Green Fees: $8 - $20 • Golf Carts: not available
Open daily 7:00 a.m. - 5:00 p.m. • Tee times: required on weekends

**Kalakaua Golf Course**
USASCH, Scholfield Barracks, Hawaii 96857 • (808) 655-9833
Military • 18 Holes • Par 72
Green Fees: $18 public (military guest) • Golf Carts: $10 (optional)
Open daily 6:30 a.m. - sunset
Tee times: required three days in advance

**Kaneohe Klipper Golf Course**
Kaneohe MCAS, Kaneohe Bay, Hawaii 96863 • (808) 254-2107
Military • 18 Holes • Par 72
Green Fees: $22 public (military guest) • Golf Carts: $15 (optional)
Open daily 6:30 a.m. - sunset • Tee times: requested

**Ko Olina Golf Course**
3733 Alii Dr., West Beach, Hawaii 96707 • (808) 676-5300
Resort • 18 Holes • Par 72
Green Fees: $95 • Golf Carts: included (mandatory)
Open daily 6:30 a.m. - 6:30 p.m. • Tee times: required

**Leilehua Golf Course**
USASCH Schofield Barracks, Hawaii 96857 • (808) 655-4653
Military • 18 Holes • Par 72
Green Fees: $23 public (military guest) • Golf Carts: $10 (optional)
Open daily 7:30 a.m. - sunset • Tee times: required

**Makaha Valley Country Club**
84/627 Makaha Valley Rd., Waianae, Hawaii 96792 • (808)695-7111
Public • 18 Holes • Par 71
Green Fees: $30 - $70 • Golf Carts: included (mandatory)
Open daily 6:40 a.m. - 6:30 p.m. • Tee times: advised

**Ted Makalena Golf Course**
93-059 Waipio Pt. Access Rd., Waipahu, Hawaii 96797 • (808) 296-7888
Municipal • 18 Holes • Par 71
Green Fees: $6 - $12 • Golf Carts: $11 (optional)
Open daily 6:00 a.m. - 6:00 p.m.
Tee times: required one week in advance

**Mid-Pacific Country Club**
266 Kaelepulu Dr., Kailua, Hawaii 96734 • (808) 261-9765
Private • 18 Holes • Par 72
Green Fees: $143 (non-members) • Golf Carts: $7 (mandatory)
Open daily 7:00 a.m. - 6:00 p.m. • Tee times: required

**Mililani Golf Course**
95-176 Kuahelani Ave., Mililani, Hawaii 96789 • (808) 623-2254
Public • 18 Holes • Par 72
Green Fees: $33 - $80 • Golf Carts: included (mandatory)
Open daily sunrise to sunset • Tee times: required

**Moanalua Golf Club**
1250 Ala Aolani St., Honolulu, Hawaii 96819 • (808) 839-2411
Semi-Private • 9 Holes • Par 36
Green Fees: $15 - $25 • Golf Carts: $9 (optional)
Open daily sunrise to sunset • Tee times: may be reserved

**Walter Nagorski Golf Course**
USASCH, Bldg. 716, Fort Shafter, Hawaii 96858 • (808) 438-9587
Military • 9 Holes • Par 34
Green Fees: $13 public (military guest) • Golf Carts: $5 - $10 (optional)
Open daily 7:30 a.m. - sunset • Tee times: requested

**Navy-Marine Golf Course**
Bldg. 43, Valkenburgh St., Honolulu, Hawaii 96818 • (808) 471-0142
Military • 18 Holes • Par 72
Green Fees: vary (military guest)
Golf Carts: $12 military, $20 guest (optional)
Open daily 7:00 a.m. to 6:30 p.m. • Tee times: required

**Oahu Country Club**
150 Country Club Rd., Honolulu, Hawaii 96817 • (808) 595-3256
Private • 18 Holes • Par 72
Green Fees: $19 - $43.25 • Golf Carts: $7 (optional)
Open daily 7:00 a.m. - sunset
Tee times: required one week in advance

**Olomana Golf Links**
41-1801 Kalanianaole Hwy., Waimanalo, Hawaii 96795 • (808) 259-7926
Public • 18 Holes • Par 72
Green Fees: $29 - $65 • Golf Carts: included (mandatory)
Open daily 7:00 a.m. - sunset
Tee times: required (may be made up to one month in advance)

**Pali Golf Course**
45-050 Kamehameha Hwy., Kaneohe, Hawaii 96744 • (808) 296-7254
Municipal • 18 Holes • Par 72
Green Fees: $8 - $18 • Golf Carts: $11 (optional)
Open daily 6:00 a.m. - 6:00 p.m.
Tee times: required one week in advance

**Pearl Country Club**
98-535 Kaonohi St., Aiea, Hawaii 96701 • (808) 487-3802
Public • 18 Holes • Par 72
Green Fees: $35 - $75 • Golf Carts: included (mandatory)
Open daily 7:00 a.m. - sunset
Tee times: required (may be made up to one month in advance)

**Sheraton Makaha Resort and Country Club**
84-626 Makaha Valley Rd., Waianae, Hawaii 96792 • (808) 695-9544
Resort • 18 Holes • Par 72
Green Fees: $65 - $135 • Golf Carts: included (mandatory)
Open daily 7:00 a.m. - 6:00 p.m. • Tee times: required

**Turtle Bay Country Club**
P.O. Box 187, Kahuku, Hawaii 96731 • (808) 293-8574
Resort • 18 Holes • Par 72
Green Fees: $67.50 - $99 • Golf Carts: included (mandatory)
Open daily 7:00 a.m. - sunset
Tee times: required (may be made up to one month in advance)

**Waialae Country Club**
4997 Kahala Ave., Honolulu, Hawaii 96816 • (808) 732-1457
Private • 18 Holes • Par 72
Green Fees: vary, guests must be sponsored by a member
Golf Carts: available • Open daily • Tee times: required

**West Loch Municipal Golf Course**
911126 Okupe Street, Ewa Beach, Hawaii 96706 • (808) 676-2210
Municipal • 18 Holes • Par 72
Green Fees: $8 - $20 • Golf Carts: $11 (optional)
Open daily 6:00 a.m. - 6:00 p.m. • Tee times: requested

## Island of Molokai

**Ironwood Hills Golf Course**
P.O. Box 8, Kualapuu, Hawaii 96757 • (808) 567-6000
Public • 9 Holes • Par 35
Green Fees: $3 - $10 • Golf Carts: $7 - $10 (optional)
Open daily 7:00 a.m. - 6:00 p.m. • Tee times: advised

**Kaluakoi Golf Course**
P.O. Box 26, Maunaloa, Hawaii 96770 • (808) 552-2739
Resort • 18 Holes • Par 72
Green Fees: $50 - $70 • Golf Carts: included (mandatory)
Open daily 7:00 a.m. - 6:30 p.m. • Tee times: required

## Island of Lanai

**The Experience at Koele**
P.O. Box "L", Lanai City, Hawaii 96763 • (808) 565-7233
Resort • 18 Holes • Par 72
Green Fees: $75 - $130 • Golf Carts: included
Open daily 7:00 a.m. - 6:00 p.m. • Tee times: required

**The Challenge at Manele** (Opening early 1993)
P.O. Box "L", Lanai City, Hawaii 96763 • (808) 565-7233
Resort • 18 Holes • Par 72
Green Fees: $75 - $130 • Golf Carts: included
Open daily 7:00 a.m. - 6:00 p.m. • Tee times: required

**Cavendish Golf Course**
P.O. Box 862, Lanai City, Hawaii 96763 • (808) 565-7044
Public • 9 Holes • Par 36

## Island of Maui

**Kaanapali North Course**
Kaanapali Beach Resort, Lahaina, Hawaii 96761 • (808) 661-3691
Resort • 18 Holes • Par 72
Green Fees: $50 - $100 • Golf Carts: included (mandatory)
Open daily 7:00 a.m. - 5:00 p.m. • Tee times: required

**Kaanapali South Course**
Kaanapali Beach Resort, Lahaina, Hawaii 96761 • (808) 661-3691
Resort • 18 Holes • Par 72
Green Fees: $50 - $100 • Golf Carts: included (mandatory)
Open daily 7:00 a.m. - 5:00 p.m. • Tee times: required

**Kapalua Bay Course**
300 Kapalua Drive, Lahaina, Hawaii 96761 • (808) 669-8044
Resort • 18 Holes • Par 72
Green Fees: $60 - $90 • Golf Carts: $15 per person (mandatory)
Open daily 6:00 a.m. - 6:30 p.m. • Tee times: required

**Kapalua Plantation Golf Club**
300 Kapalua Drive, Lahaina, Hawaii 96761 • (808) 669-8044
Resort • 18 Holes • Par 72
Green Fees: $60 - $90 • Golf Carts: $15 per person (mandatory)
Open daily • Tee times: required

**Kapalua Village Course**
300 Kapalua Drive, Lahaina, Hawaii 96761 • (808) 669-8044
Resort • 18 Holes • Par 72
Green Fees: $60 - $90 • Golf Carts: $15 per person (mandatory)
Open daily 6:00 a.m. - 6:30 p.m. • Tee times: required

**Makena Resort Golf Course**
5415 Makena Alanui, Kihei, Hawaii 96753 • (808) 879-3344
Resort • 18 Holes • Par 72
Green Fees: $55 - $100 • Golf Carts: included (mandatory)
Open daily 6:30 a.m. - 6:15 pm. • Tee times: required

**Maui Country Club**
48 Nonohe Place, Paia, Hawaii 96779 • (808) 877-7893
Private • 9 Holes • Par 37
Green Fees: guests must be sponsored by a member
Golf Carts: available (optional) • Open daily 6:30 a.m. - 6:30 p.m.
Tee times: required

**Pukalani Country Club**
360 Pukalani Street, Pukalani, Hawaii 96768 • (808) 572-1314
Public • 18 Holes • Par 72
Green Fees: $32 - $43 • Golf Carts: $12 (mandatory)
Open daily 7:00 a.m. - 6:00 p.m. • Tee times: required

**Silversword Golf Course**
1345 Piilani Highway, Kihei, Hawaii 96753 • (808) 874-0777
Public • 18 Holes • Par 71
Green Fees: $27 - $60 • Golf Carts: included (mandatory)
Open daily 6:30 a.m. - 6:00 p.m. • Tee times: required

**Waiehu Golf Course**
P.O. Box 507, Wailuku, Hawaii 96796 • (808) 244-5934
Municipal • 18 Holes • Par 72
Green Fees: $5 - $25 • Golf Carts: $6.50 (optional)
Open daily 7:00 a.m. - 5:00 p.m. • Tee times: required

**Wailea Golf Club, Blue Course**
120 Kaukahi Street, Wailea, Hawaii 96753-8493 • (808) 879-2966
Resort • 18 Holes • Par 72
Green Fees: $65 - $115 • Golf Carts: included (mandatory)
Open daily 6:30 a.m. - 6:30 p.m. • Tee times: required

**Wailea Golf Club, Orange Course**
120 Kaukahi Street, Wailea, Hawaii 96753-8493 • (808) 879-2966
Resort • 18 Holes • Par 72
Green Fees: $65 - $115 • Golf Carts: included (mandatory)
Open daily 6:30 a.m. - 6:30 p.m. • Tee times: required

## Island of Hawaii

**Discovery Harbour Golf & Country Club**
P.O. Box Q, Naalehu, Hawaii 96772 • (808) 929-7353
Public • 18 Holes • Par 72
Green Fees: $10 • Golf Carts: $14 (optional)
Open daily 7:30 a.m. - 3:30 p.m. • Tee times: not required

**Hamakua Country Club**
P.O. Box 751, Honokaa, Hawaii 96727 • (808) 775-7380
Public • 9 Holes • Par 33
Green Fees: $10 • Golf Carts: not available
Open weekdays only, sunrise - sunset • Tee times: not required

**Hilo Municipal Golf Course**
340 Haihai St., Hilo, Hawaii 96720 • (808) 959-7711
Municipal • 18 Holes • Par 71
Green Fees: $4 - $8 • Golf Carts: $14 (optional)
Open daily 7:00 a.m. - 5:00 p.m.
Tee times: required for weekends, may be made a week in advance

**Kona Country Club**
78-7000 Alii Dr., Kailua-Kona, Hawaii 96740 • (808) 322-2595
Resort • 27 Holes • Par 72
Green Fees: $70 - $100 • Golf Carts: included (mandatory)
Open daily 6:45 a.m. - sunset
Tee times: required, may be made 3 days in advance

**Mauna Kea Golf Course**
One Mauna Kea Beach Dr., Kohala Coast, Hawaii 96743 • (808) 882-7222
Resort • 18 Holes • Par 72
Green Fees: $75 - $125 • Golf Carts: included (mandatory)
Open daily 7:00 a.m. - 6:00 p.m. • Tee times: required

**Mauna Lani Resort (Francis H. I'i Brown Golf Course)**
P.O. Box 4959, Kohala Coast, Hawaii 96743 • (808) 885-6655
Resort • 18 Holes • Par 72
Green Fees: $65 - $130 • Golf Carts: included (mandatory)
Open daily 6:00 a.m. - 6:00 p.m. • Tee times: required

**Naniloa Country Club**
120 Banyan Drive, Hilo, Hawaii 96720 • (808) 935-3000
Semi-Private • 9 Holes • Par 35
Green Fees: $25 - $35 • Golf Carts: $14 (optional)
Open daily 7:00 a.m. - 4:30 p.m.
Tee times: required weekends and holidays

**Volcano Golf and Country Club**
P.O. Box 46, Volcano National Park, Hawaii 96718 • (808) 967-7331
Public • 18 Holes • Par 72
Green Fees: $21 - $35 • Golf Carts: included (mandatory)
Open daily 7:00 a.m. - 2:30 p.m. • Tee times: required

**Waikoloa Beach Course**
P.O. Box 5100, Waikoloa, Hawaii 96743 • (808) 885-6060
Resort • 18 Holes • Par 70
Green Fees: $70 - $90 • Golf Carts: included (mandatory)
Open daily 7:00 a.m. - 6:00 p.m. • Tee times: recommended

**Waikoloa King's Course**
P.O. Box 5575, Waikoloa, Hawaii 96743 • (808) 885-4647
Resort • 18 Holes • Par 72
Green Fees: $80 - $95 • Golf Carts: included (mandatory)
Open daily 7:00 a.m. - 6:00 p.m. • Tee times: recommended

**Waikoloa Village Course**
P.O. Box 3008, Waikoloa, Hawaii 96743 • (808) 883-9621
Resort • 18 Holes • Par 72
Green Fees: $35 - $60 • Golf Carts: included (mandatory)
Open daily 7:00 a.m. - 6:30 p.m.
Tee times: required, may be made 48 hours in advance

Additional Photo Credits...

Pages 50 & 51, Tomas del Amo; page 106, George Fuller; pages 116 & 117 provided by Rockresorts, Inc.; pages 166, 167, 168 & 169, William Waterfall; page 192 provided by Hyatt Regency Waikoloa